Francisco de Vitoria and the Evolution of International Law

Francisco de Vitoria and the Evolution of International Law

Justifying Injustice

Amaya Amell

LEXINGTON BOOKS
Lanham • Boulder • New York • London

Published by Lexington Books
An imprint of The Rowman & Littlefield Publishing Group, Inc.
4501 Forbes Boulevard, Suite 200, Lanham, Maryland 20706
www.rowman.com

6 Tinworth Street, London SE11 5AL, United Kingdom

British Library Cataloguing in Publication Information Available

Library of Congress Cataloging-in-Publication Data

Names: Amell, Amaya, author.
Title: Francisco de Vitoria and the evolution of international law : justifying injustice / Amaya Amell.
Description: Lanham, Maryland : published by Lexington Books, an imprint of The Rowman & Littlefield Publishing Group, Inc., [2021] | Includes bibliographical references and index. | Summary: "This book is a reconstruction of the philosophical and legal theories of Fray Francisco de Vitoria, one of the primary founders of international law, and how these served to introduce the theory of an international community in which all nations take part, regardless of religious beliefs"—Provided by publisher.
Identifiers: LCCN 2020050346 (print) | LCCN 2020050347 (ebook) | ISBN 9781793613349 (cloth) | ISBN 9781793613356 (epub)
Subjects: LCSH: Vitoria, Francisco de, 1486?-1546. | International law—Philosophy.
Classification: LCC KZ2159 .A64 2021 (print) | LCC KZ2159 (ebook) | DDC 341.01—dc23
LC record available at https://lccn.loc.gov/2020050346
LC ebook record available at https://lccn.loc.gov/2020050347

Contents

Introduction

Legitimizing the Illegitimate

Since the beginning of civilization, theologians, philosophers, jurists, and other intellectuals have dedicated time and effort to evaluating and reevaluating the concepts of international law, human rights, and just war. In doing so, they have given scholars of today a look at the progression of liberal ideals throughout history and shown the tenacity of traditional values as well as the difficulties encountered when attempting to alter the status quo, even though the history of human rights encompasses thousands of years and is modified each time there is a new cultural, legal, religious, or philosophical development. The following are some notable human rights documents recorded throughout history: The Cyrus Cylinder of 539 B.C., in which Cyrus the Great declares his intentions after the conquest of the neo-Babylonian Empire; The Constitution of Medina of A.D. 622, created by Muhammed as a type of behavioral agreement between various tribes of Medina including Muslims and Jews; and the English Magna Carta of 1215, which is especially important in the history of Western law.

Is the history of the Spanish conquest of the Americas one of unjust war, illegal invasion of foreign territories, and the violation of human rights? Were the subsequent attempts to right the previously committed wrongs just a political move for the sake of self-justification in the face of international scrutiny? Was the debate between Fray Bartolomé de las Casas and Juan Ginés de Sepúlveda a battle of suppressors, one in the name of divine law and the other in the name of natural law? Or was the development of laws to protect the American Indians from abuse an unprecedented attempt to follow the divine law to "love thy neighbor as thyself"? From our present point of view, with our 20/20 hindsight of colonial imperialism and our present-day politics of invasions of foreign territories in the name of social justice, one may be inclined to render the verdict contained in the beginning sentence.

But does this 20/20 hindsight really exist? Is not all that is known about history a series of accounts rendered by eyewitnesses, who told their part of the story, according to what they had experienced and therefore partial and subjective? Have politics not always been a matter of trying to find the right balance between doing what is deemed best for one's own particular interests and "the greater good," while maintaining a delicate balance of powers with other countries?

There are various historical approaches to the subject of international law and human rights in the context of the Spanish conquest of the Americas. This book examines the evolution of the theory of international law by focusing on the conquest of the Americas as a crucial moment of reassessment of human rights. The impact of the conquest of the Americas, an encounter with a totally different world, ultimately resulted in a rearticulation of the Old World's preconceived notions about human nature and the rights of people and nations. This relationship between colonial expansion and the law of nations was at the center of many of the discussions that took place throughout Spain and the New World by intellectuals, jurists, and theologians in an attempt to find a way to reconcile these two often contradictory notions. A prominent scholar of the School of Salamanca, who addressed this conflictive relationship extensively and was hailed by many as one of the founders of international law, was Francisco de Vitoria.

This book discusses the lectures of sixteenth-century theologian Francisco de Vitoria and compares his thoughts to those of Hugo Grotius and John Locke, in order to present a better perspective on the issues of natural, human, and divine law and their evolution through time. It also brings to light the paradoxes and contradictions inherent in the abovementioned theories and their application. Vitoria's ideas, as well as those of Grotius and Locke, contributed significantly to future debates and discussions on the philosophy of law, the evolution of international law, just war theory, and human rights.

The abovementioned prominent figures were each in their own way committed to the advancement of the theories of natural law, *jus gentium* (law of nations), and *bellum justum* (just war) by breaking away from preestablished norms. In questioning and reexamining traditional ideas about these concepts, they have been able to redefine the notion of human rights that had once been intrinsic in the Roman canon of law and present a more naturalistic concept of power and its moral limitations. This shift in perspective was a sign of the times: the end of the Middle Ages followed by the Renaissance and the Age of Enlightenment.

I will provide a critical and systematic reconstruction of Vitoria's philosophical and legal theories and will analyze his thoughts as expressed in his lectures, and which were revolutionary at the time, and show how these served to introduce the theory of an international community: a community in which all nations take part. Given Francisco de Vitoria's background, his political philosophy must be viewed within his theories on law and powers of the state and church. I therefore focus primarily on two of Vitoria's lectures, "On the Indians (De Indis)" and "On the Law of War (De Jure Belli)," to discuss his views on divine, natural, and human law; the concepts of church, nation, state, just war, and human rights; and the legitimizing process involved in the encounter between colonizers and the indigenous people. The conquest of the Americas and the reevaluation of previous concepts that it entailed resulted in the establishment of the fundamental theories of international law, just war, and human rights that are still in effect today.

I chose this topic because I strongly admire Vitoria's endeavor, unique at the time, to create a moral philosophy that would incorporate an interpretation of the classic Roman laws in a discourse that would center primarily not on divine law but on natural law, a law that would always apply equally to every person, culture, and nation.

Chapter 1 presents a look at the life and education of Fray Francisco de Vitoria in order to offer insight into the background from which he formed his thoughts, which were groundbreaking for his time. In chapter 2 Vitoria's theories on law, its hierarchy and powers, and the powers of the state and the church are analyzed in order to achieve a better understanding of his concept of human rights, *bellum justum* (just war), and *jus gentium* (law of nations). Chapter 3 discusses the rights of the American Indians and illustrates Vitoria's fundamental notions on law, church, and state, which together formulate his concept of human rights. Chapter 4 discusses Vitoria's *relectio* on just war to reconstruct his theory and the legitimate reasons that he proposed for the Spanish invasion of the Americas, using the traditional just war theory and its definition presented by St. Augustine. Chapter 5 deals with the concept of law and just war in Huig de Groot, or Hugo Grotius as he is most commonly known. I have included this and the following chapter on John Locke in order to illustrate how much of Vitoria's ideas found resonance in the writings of his successors and how his proposed shift from divine law to natural law continued to develop after his time.

In order to better understand the strong impetus that was felt to reinvent the conventional notions of law during the conquest and post-conquest in Spain, it is essential to examine the background against which these ideas were developed and the global challenges that Spain faced from rising European competition and questions about American Indian sovereignty.

During the sixteenth century, there were several attempts made by the Crown to find the right, "morally just" means of governing its new overseas empire and its subjects. The conquest of the Americas with all its complexities forced the Spanish Crown to focus for the first time on the question of human rights and colonial order. It looked mainly to theologians to answer the questions regarding the righteousness of the decisions being made and actions being taken with respect to the New World. Spain was, after all, being closely scrutinized by its English and French competitors, who were ready to criticize and use to their advantage any unjust action it might take as proof that the Spanish Crown was not worthy of the mission entrusted to it by Pope Alexander VI in his Bulls of Donation issued in May 1493. As a result, no other European nation, except possibly Portugal, took its Christian duty toward the native inhabitants as seriously as Spain.

During this time, theologians proposed possible solutions to problems encountered in the New World, with full approval of the Crown. They attempted to provide answers for the following questions: Could or should the American Indians learn to live like Spaniards? Would it be possible to colonize new lands peacefully with Spanish farmers? Could the American Indians be won over to Christianity by peaceful means alone? Could the encomienda (tribute and forced labor) system be abolished? In the end, it turned out to be impossible to put these theories into practice, mainly because of the opposition they received from the majority of the colonizers. Nevertheless, it is crucial to take notice of the fact that these efforts were made at all, especially by one of the most powerful military empires during an era of territorial expansion.

The influence that those humanitarians exerted on the Crown and the decision-making process regarding the New World is evident. The strong conviction of those who believed that the conquest of the New World could be successfully achieved without disrespecting the natives' rights as human beings was an extraordinary phenomenon during this time. Successful and sincere or not, these attempts serve to demonstrate the Spanish Empire's preoccupation with finding the best legal and theological approach to the treatment of the American Indians, while creating an impressive colonial order in light of the possible encroachment by other European colonizers.

One of the pioneers in the defense of the American Indians' human rights was Fray Antonio de Montesinos. In 1511, this Dominican friar delivered one of the most influential and powerful sermons in Conquest history addressing the following question: On which authority had the Spanish Crown waged such a violent war against these harmless people in their own land? In his sermon, Montesinos rebuked the Spanish colonists' dehumanized view and treatment of the natives. He made it clear that the American Indians were human beings, not barbarians, and therefore fully capable of assimilating the Christian religion. Montesinos warned the encomenderos (land owners) and conquistadores (conquerors) that they were in a state of mortal sin and questioned the authority that would allow such horrible things to be done to a peaceful people.

Although Montesinos did not necessarily question the legitimacy of the Spanish dominion in the New World, he did severely criticize not only the abusive behavior of the Spanish settlers toward the American Indians but also their failure to convert them, as was intended with the encomienda system. His ideas clashed drastically with the interests of the encomenderos. Here emerges the beginning of the sharp division between spiritual and material objectives that became a part of the post-Conquest era: the battle between the Dominican followers of Montesinos and the colonizers of the New World protecting their own material interests.

King Ferdinand was surprised when he heard about Montesinos's public protest against the treatment of the American Indians by the Spaniards. Until then, the basis for Spanish rule in the Americas had been justified by the assignment of territories by Pope Alexander VI under the Bulls of Donation, which was considered to be in accordance with human and divine law. As Lewis Hanke states, "Up to the time when Montesinos lifted his voice in Hispaniola, every Spaniard high and low believed that the Pope had granted the newly-discovered lands to their kings and had charged them to convert the Indians" (Hanke 1974, 26). Montesinos's sermon forced the Spanish Crown to reexamine its claim to sovereignty in the New World and view the traditionally idealized heroic conqueror in a different light.

As a result, in 1512 King Ferdinand called forth an assembly of counselors in Burgos in order to discuss the frequent denunciations of Spanish abuse of the American Indians that the Crown had received. Friar Antonio de Montesinos went to speak for the Dominicans, whereas the Spanish colonists sent Franciscan friar Alonso Espinal as their representative. The *Junta de Burgos* (Burgos Congress) was led by the bishop of Palencia, Juan Rodríguez de Fonseca. This was the first time the Spanish Crown called together a meeting of theologians for an official discussion of the problems encountered in the New World. On December 27, 1512, the outcome of these discussions was embodied in the Laws of Burgos and became the first comprehensive code of American Indian legislation, setting rules for the behavior of the Spanish settlers in the New World with regards to the native population, although these rules were sadly not genuinely followed. Nevertheless, the Laws of Burgos were important in their attempt to impose rules of moral conduct on the Spanish conquerors and settlers in the Americas. They forbade the maltreatment of the American Indians and endorsed their conversion to Christianity above all else. However, they not only failed to recognize the freedom of the American Indians and their right to be treated as equals but also concluded that they must be subject to coercion and kept under the eye of the Spaniards in order for a successful conversion to take place. According to these laws, the encomienda, was deemed a just method by the Crown.

These laws were very poorly applied in the New World, and in 1513, the king ordered a committee of theologians to study the American Indian problem again. The deliberations of this committee brought forth the enforcement of the *Requerimiento*, written by Juan López de Palacios Rubios. This was a declaration of Spanish sovereignty read by the conquistadores in the name of King Ferdinand V as defender of the Catholic Church to assert his authority and control over the New World in God's name. It was used to justify the claim that God was the ruler of the whole world and that by the Papal Bull of Pope Alexander VI the Spaniards had a legitimate title of sovereignty over all of the Americas. The conquistadores were expected to read this document aloud to the natives and get their response to it before starting any kind of aggressive action. It did not work as expected for many reasons, the most important of which was that the American Indians obviously could not understand what was being read to them and therefore did not have any response. It was not taken very seriously by the Spanish conquistadores either, and it turned out to be just a facade rather than a sincere attempt at helping the American Indians understand what was happening.

Although the results of the *Leyes de Burgos* (Laws of Burgos) and of the *Requerimiento* were not as expected, they did serve to illustrate that the sermons preached by Montesinos had at least disturbed the court and had served as a catalyst for future actions taken by the Crown concerning the American Indians. Measures were being taken, or at least attempted, by the Crown to reduce the abuse of the natives and protect their well-being, albeit in order to maximize their efficiency as a work force above all else.

After the conquest of Mexico (1520–1522) and Peru (1531–2532) the discussion of the proper treatment of the American Indians reached its climax. In 1524, another council dealing specifically with the American Indians was created, the *Consejo de Indias* (Council of the Indies), whose decisions became the basis for the New Laws of 1542, again designed to protect the American Indians' human rights, but with seemingly more detail and force.

The New Laws were created for the protection and well-being of the American Indians, the establishment of a colonial order, and the abolishment of the encomienda system in an attempt to stop the abuse and exploitation endured by the natives at the hands of the Spaniards, especially from the encomenderos (land owners). The New Laws ordered that the American Indians would no longer be at the mercy of the encomenderos and could not be made slaves. A new system of labor distribution, known as the *repartimiento*, was established. This system allocated a certain number of American Indians to the encomenderos under terms of service that included better treatment and a salary. Although in theory this salary was what most differentiated the *repartimiento* system from the encomienda, the American Indians were also then expected to pay a tribute to the Crown as "loyal vassals," which meant that they ended up giving most of their hard-earned salary right back to the Crown. Also, even though according to the *repartimiento* system the American Indians were supposed to receive better treatment, in reality this was not the case and they were still treated harshly by their abusers. The hypocrisy of the government once again was apparent: the *repartimiento* system was created not necessarily for the well-being of the American Indians, as it claimed to be, but rather as a way to keep the American Indian labor force more apt to work for the Crown.

The New Laws did aim at eventually abolishing the whole encomienda system and ordered officials of the Crown or clergymen with encomienda grants to hand them over immediately to the Crown. Bartolomé de las Casas, who had led the reform movement that resulted in the *Leyes de Burgos* and was infuriated with the results, had convinced Charles V to abolish the encomienda system, which in Las Casas's opinion was an exercise in futility and a continuing disregard for humanity. Under the New Laws, encomienda grants would no longer be passed on hereditarily but would be nullified at the death of the encomendero. However, the following year some of these laws were revoked in favor of the colonizers, due to the number of obstacles they faced. Their demise was assured from the beginning. On October 20, 1545, thirty rules under the New Laws were revoked, the encomienda system was no longer in danger, and the colonists were pacified, for the time being at least. In reality, this was simply a temporary solution and many questions had still been left unanswered.

The New Laws were enforced by the first viceroy of Peru, Blasco Nuñez Vela. This unfortunate man had the task of making sure that the regulations of the encomienda system were carried out, especially the prohibition of the sale of American Indians as slaves or sending them to work in the deadly mines, unless it was "absolutely necessary," and then they should be "paid fairly" and "treated respectfully." But who decided what could be defined as "absolutely necessary" and "paid fairly"? These are examples of ambiguous language being used to justify and manipulate a situation to one's own advantage. Thus, in the end, the American Indians were still being sent to the mines, simply under different pretexts.

Many colonizers were against the New Laws, because they limited the Spaniards' rights to extract service or tribute from the American Indians. They had made sure that their disagreement was duly noted by the Crown from the beginning and resolved to make it basically impossible for the New Laws to work. On their part, the friars wrote to the king about the encomenderos' rebellion against the New Laws, their refusal to abide by them, and how they continued to mistreat the American Indian population. These letters from opposing sides all urged the king to take measures. This illustrates how well-intentioned but unrealistic plans to improve the conditions of the natives backfired, primarily because of the lack of proper official enforcement. The Crown and its officials became alarmed and were convinced that this reform would not be beneficial to the new colonies and that the abolition of the encomienda system would in the end lead to economic disaster. The Crown therefore watered down the New Laws significantly and restored the encomiendas for fear of losing control over the colonies. The encomienda would not be formally abolished until the eighteenth century and played a primary role in the destruction and disintegration of the indigenous population of the Americas.

It is clear that, although the question of how to treat the natives already arose as early as 1493, it was not until the revocation of the New Laws that this issue was given the real importance that it deserved. Since the Council of the Indies was unable to reach a definitive conclusion, they turned to two of the most influential intellectuals to hear both sides of the situation. This dispute occurred at the highest level of governance and was not only sanctioned but commissioned by the Spanish monarchs.

The debate between Juan Ginés de Sepúlveda and Bartolomé de las Casas was the first held by a colonizing nation to determine the methods that were to be used to govern its overseas territories and inhabitants, methods that were "morally justifiable." The philosopher Eduardo Andújar describes the debate between Sepúlveda and Las Casas as "the clearest instance of an imperial power openly questioning the legitimacy of its rights and the ethical basis of its political actions" (Andújar 1997, 8). What type of humans were the Indians if they were human at all? Did they possess the ability to learn and assimilate Christianity and European civilization? These questions were at the base of the debate between Las Casas and Sepúlveda in 1550, which put two conflicting interpretations of Christianity face to face. The debate produced a conflict between two historical forces: pagan culturalist elitism, which would refer to Sepúlveda's position, and Christian metaphysical egalitarianism, which underlies Las Casas's ideology. Sepúlveda stressed the cultural difference between the Europeans and the Indians, whereas Las Casas sought to minimize it. A point worth mentioning here is that, while many believe that Montesinos's sermon profoundly touched Las Casas and inspired him to change his direction in life, this was not the case. A year after the sermon, Las Casas participated in the conquest of Cuba and held an encomienda. It was not until 1514 that he began to contemplate his life, and it was not until 1515 that he gave up his encomienda and began to dedicate his life to protecting the American Indians and defending their rights.

Although many authors have claimed that Sepúlveda's doctrine was less favorably considered than Las Casas's, this was not entirely true. Sepúlveda's perspective triumphed with those whose interests he represented: the colonizers and the soldiers. He wanted to demonstrate that the war against the American Indians was a preliminary action necessary for their full conversion to Christianity. Las Casas opposed Sepúlveda's position and wrote his manuscript, *Apología*, arguing against everything that Sepúlveda declared in his work, *Sumario*. The sessions of the debate began in Valladolid in August 1550 and continued for about a month in front of the Council of the Fourteen, a council that was commissioned by King Charles V to determine if there was justice or not in the war with the American Indians and the best way to convert them to Christianity. On the first day, Sepúlveda spoke for three hours, giving a summary of his work. On the second day, Las Casas appeared with his entire manuscript and read it chapter by chapter, a lengthy, drawn-out process which lasted five days. He responded point by point to Sepúlveda's declarations in his manuscript, *Sumario*, a summary of his *Democrates Alter*.

In defense of the American Indians, Las Casas highly praised their ability in things that were also part of the European civilized world, such as logic, grammar, music, writing, and art. Sepúlveda argued that the artistic ability of the American Indians was not demonstrative of their capacity for civilization, because animals could also construct impressive works of art. Las Casas fired back that this was nonsense and that Sepúlveda should have consulted with those who had lived among the American Indians and knew their way of life firsthand before making those ridiculous statements. Las Casas said that once the American Indians were taught the Christian doctrine in a peaceful manner, they would open up their hearts to the new religion and embrace it wholeheartedly, because they were not barbaric and ignorant but sincere and simple people. He added that the great Aztec and Incan empires were in their final stages before the "coming of the faith." This was another reason why the Spaniards had no need to persecute the American Indians with violent means.

Sepúlveda's first reason as to why the war against the natives was justified was that the American Indians of the New World were at such an advanced level of barbarism that for their own good it was necessary to force them out of this condition. Las Casas argued that one cannot mention barbarism in such a vague manner. He found that, according to Aristotle's ideas on barbarism, there were different levels and types of barbarians. First, there were those who engaged in barbaric behavior, a good example of which were the Spanish colonizers and their vicious treatment of the American Indians. Second, there existed those who were barbarians due to their lack of written language. Las Casas assured that this was not the case with the American Indians, because missionaries in the New World, before and after Las Casas, had expressed their admiration for the complexity and beauty of the indigenous language. Last, there were those who were barbarians by nature. Las Casas said that these types were like freaks of nature, and God would surely not have interfered with his plan for all mankind to have a rational nature by making an immense population of irrational creatures.

Sepúlveda's second argument was that the war against the American Indians could be justified because they committed acts against natural law, such as cannibalism, idolatry, and human sacrifice. Las Casas opposed this argument and stated that since the Spaniards did not possess jurisdiction over the American Indians in this respect, they could not punish them. A point of view that Las Casas shared with prominent intellectuals, such as Vitoria, was that the Jews and the Moors, who lived in Spain and who had to obey the Christian prince because they were under temporal jurisdiction, did not have to obey in spiritual matters. Las Casas said that the only ones who could be punished for idolatry were those who turned their back on the promise they had made to God and the church during baptism. Therefore, since the American Indians had never heard the word of God until the arrival of the Spaniards, they actually had sinned less than the Jews, due to their ignorance. If the Spanish Church could not punish the Jews in Spain for their lack of Christian faith (it could "officially" only punish the *converts*), then why would they be able to punish idolaters who had never heard of the Christian religion before?

Sepúlveda's third reason for the war against the American Indians was that they oppressed innocent people and sacrificed them to their gods, and this was against natural law, to which all are subject. Interestingly, Las Casas agreed with him on this basic premise, but he argued that the American Indians did not do these actions against natural law. If the American Indians killed Christians and preachers, they did not kill them because they were preachers or Christians but because they were seen by the American Indians as enemies who tortured, mistreated, and killed them. Las Casas did always support and believe in the just war against the Saracens and Turks, as did Vitoria, but he argued that the American Indians were in a totally different category because their resistance was purely defensive. Although Las Casas did not agree with the American Indians' acts of human sacrifice, he believed that in some cases, such as these, it would be better to tolerate the deaths of a few innocents if that would eventually lead to the salvation of a larger amount of people. Las Casas added a thought-provoking twist to this argument: human sacrifice must not be *that* bad in the eyes of God, since He Himself ordered Abraham to sacrifice his only son to Him. Here, he illustrates the concept that human sacrifice was a horrible yet essential element in all religions.

Sepúlveda's fourth and last argument was that the war against the "infidels" was necessary to pave the way for Christianity successfully. This idea is remarkably similar to that presented in the Islamic theory, according to which, contrary to what many think, especially post-9/11, jihad does not necessarily mean holy war, since the term "holy war" does not exist in the *Qur'an*. The term "jihad" is translated literally as "struggle," referring primarily to an interior struggle, even though it has been applied to an external struggle as well. There are four types of jihad to which scholars generally refer: (1) a personal, spiritual, and moral struggle within the person in order to overcome selfishness and adhere more strictly to Islamic teaching; (2) a struggle in an unbelieving society where those that have the Islamic faith are encouraged to carry out the word regardless of the resistance met; (3) a personal witness to the life and teaching of Mohammed, setting an example and encouraging others to devote their lives to the will of Allah; and finally, (4) an exterior holy war against those who persecute the followers of Islam and impede the spreading of the Islamic faith.[1] This last reference is the one that most closely reflects the idea of Sepúlveda, and Vitoria, that war may be justified when it is waged against those who impede the spread of the Christian faith. However, Las Casas vehemently opposed use of force as a means of conversion. Did the Scripture proclaim that Christianity should be preached with violence? What good would come from this? The only thing that would happen would be that the American Indians would come to hate those who brought with them the word of God. They would associate this new religion with oppression and suffering. If this were to occur, Las Casas claimed, the results could be disastrous. Also, referring again directly to the Scriptures, Las Casas made sure to remind his audience that Christ never armed his disciples so they could teach better. On the contrary, he scolded Peter for slicing off the ear of one of the soldiers who came with Judas to arrest him.

Interestingly enough, as contemporary and liberal as Las Casas's theories must sound juxtaposed to Sepúlveda's, he never questioned the legitimacy of Spanish sovereignty in the New World, just the theological and political forces behind this power. Also, his concept of the American Indians' liberty was that true freedom could only be obtained by entirely giving up their former way of life and by becoming completely subservient to the church. His defense for the autonomy of the American Indians was based on an absolutist concept of the spiritual and temporal power of the church. As a result, his view of the liberty of the American Indian paradoxically robbed them of their own voice. The American Indians could be "free" as long as they turned themselves over to the temporal and spiritual power of the church. This viewpoint was in direct contrast with that of Vitoria, who took a more aggressive approach against the absolute power of the church. In this respect, Vitoria proved to be more trailblazing conceptually and more willing to make a break from not only the power of the church but that of the emperor as well. As Eduardo Subirats describes,

> La doctrina jurídica de Vitoria establecía por vez primera una ruptura con respecto a los ideales de cruzada que habían inspirado el descubrimiento y la conquista españoles de América. Más que Las Casas, con su ambigua defensa de las libertades del indio en nombre precisamente de su conversión y avasallamiento, era Vitoria quien con ello trazaba una definitiva línea divisora entre la concepción medieval y la concepción moderna del Nuevo Mundo. (Vitoria's judicial doctrine established for the first time a break with regard to

> the crusade-ideals that had inspired the Spanish discovery and conquest of the Americas. More than Las Casas, with his ambiguous defense of the freedom of the Indian precisely in name of their conversion and subjugation, it was Vitoria who created a definitive line dividing the medieval and modern concepts of the New World). (Subirats 2003, 384)

Unfortunately, the written accounts of the sessions of the council have been lost, so the only means that scholars have to rebuild the events of this debate are the reconstructed arguments of the two opponents by eyewitnesses such as the judges.

The conclusion of Las Casas is never in doubt: for those who had never before heard of the church or of Christianity, Sepúlveda's reasons for waging war on them were not applicable; these people were not barbarians and had their own order and civilization. Just because they were not like the Europeans did not mean that they were incompetent or ignorant and could be treated like inferior beings. Although no official, final "verdict" was reached with this debate, one can see the concern of the Spanish monarchy with regard to the treatment of the American Indians and how the debate affected royal policy. Never before until then had a growing empire questioned the legitimacy of its own actions in such an open way.

This was the setting in which Francisco de Vitoria's lectures, or *relecciones*, came to life. His lectures discussed openly the juridical and theological bases for Spanish sovereignty in the New World, and in doing so, he transformed and modernized the theological, philosophical, cultural, and political world of sixteenth-century Spain, the effects of which still reverberate today.

For Vitoria, there was never one simple, clear-cut answer to a problem or solution to an issue and for this reason he did not study things from a single perspective but rather from a broader, multifaceted one in order to make them fit better into his universal conception of the world. As a result, there are many contradictions and inconsistencies in his views on the legitimacy of the Spanish invasion of America, going all the way from considering the native people equal to their invaders, in spite of their different customs and religious beliefs, to defending the right of the invaders to subject them to their rule, under the guise of missionaries of the Catholic faith.

In spite of these inconsistencies, which may lead one to question the sincerity of some of his statements concerning the treatment of the American Indians, I do believe that his ideas played an important role in the political, theological, philosophical, and cultural world of sixteenth-century Spanish society, and that their effects can still be seen today. Influential scholars such as Annabel Brett, Brian Tierney, Quentin Skinner, and Anthony Pagden have recognized the impact of Vitoria's ideas on the development of modern constitutionalism and imperialistic discourse. In discussing and questioning the juridical and theological bases for Spanish sovereignty in the New World, Vitoria revolutionized the theories of jus gentium (law of nations) and *bellum justum* (just war) by breaking away from the norms that had once been intrinsic in the Roman canon of law.

NOTES

1. It is important to note that true jihads are never conducted against other Muslim nations and rarely, if ever, is their goal to attack and destroy non-Muslim nations. Unfortunately, today's extremist Islamic groups have given jihad a completely different meaning. Several scholars have pointed to a number of areas in Islamic thought that can easily allow for an extremist interpretation of jihad. As Halevi states, "Islamic doctrine easily lends itself to extremist cooptation. Islam divides the world into two regions: *Dar Al Harb*, or the house of war, containing all territories ruled by non-Muslims, and *Dar Al Islam*, or the house of Islam, which is destined to dominate the former. In a world groping towards planetary interconnectedness, this Islamic doctrine—which justifies the madness of holy war—must be challenged by the Muslims themselves" (Halevi 2001, 1).

Chapter 1

Vitoria

His Life and Influences

Francisco de Vitoria was born around 1483 in the town of Vitoria in the Basque province of Alava. His surname being identical to the name of the town in which he was born was not a coincidence. He was a convert at a time in Spain when being "tainted" by Jewish blood made life difficult. The Inquisition was busy trying to eliminate all Jewish influence in Spain and was not open to the idea of embracing converts, "infected" by their Jewish ancestry. While the Inquisition is often associated with Spain and Portugal, it actually made its first appearance in Rome when it was established by Pope Innocent III. Later, Pope Gregory IX used the Inquisition in 1233 to combat the heresy of a religious sect in France known as the Abilgenses. By the mid-thirteenth century, the Inquisition had become an authoritative force to be reckoned with and had spread throughout Western and Central Europe, except for England. In 1478 a papal bull was given to establish the Inquisition in Spain and in 1481 it was instituted in Castile with Tomás de Torquemada, who ironically was also a descendant of converts, as the Grand Inquisitor.

In the beginning, the Inquisition dealt only with Christian heretics and did not concern itself with other religions. However, even though the Catholic sovereigns, Isabella and Ferdinand, were surrounded by converts in the royal court, and Ferdinand himself was the grandson of a Jew, they displayed intolerance and fear of the Jews (especially toward any possibility of a united force of Jews and Moors, with the fall of Granada being so precariously close at hand). Obtaining a papal bull from Innocent VIII, the king and queen demanded that all fugitive converts be restored to the Inquisition of Spain, wherever they may be. In 1499 Pedro Sarmiento, who some may call a very fervent Catholic, wrote the *Sentencia-Estatuto*, which prohibited Jews and converts from testifying in court and from holding any governmental or ecclesiastical office. This was followed by the blood-cleansing phenomenon (*limpieza de sangre*) in the sixteenth century, which was completely anti-Semitic and more racial than religious in nature. It was not until 1808, under the brief rule of Joseph Bonaparte, that the Inquisition was temporarily abolished in Spain, only to be reinstated under Fernando VII and not fully eradicated until later in the century. Due to these extreme difficulties, it became a common custom for converts to take their surname from their birthplace.[1] This name change did not always have to do with Jewish origins, however. It was also a tradition in religious orders to adopt another name, convert or not.

Francisco de Vitoria was named after his father, and his mother was Catalina de Compludo. Vitoria's family had a good economic and moral standing in society. When he was still a child, Vitoria's family moved to Burgos, then the capital of Castile and residence of the sovereigns. Burgos would be a city of monumental importance in Vitoria's life and for the Spanish Empire in general, becoming the Spanish city that would hold meetings of the *Consejo de Indias* (Council of the Indies) starting in 1512. Vitoria was not an only child, he had an older brother, Diego, who was a member of the Dominican Order and later became prior of the cloister of San Pablo in Burgos. Following in his brother's footsteps, Vitoria entered the Dominican Order in Burgos in 1504. It was here where he became educated in humanities and mastered the Latin and Greek languages. In 1506, the Order assigned Vitoria to Sorbonne, or the school of Santiago, the college of the Dominicans in Paris. There, Vitoria resided in the Dominican convent and studied theology until 1509.

As a student, Vitoria had two advisers, each of who exerted a considerable amount of influence on him: John Fennarius and Peter Crockart. Since Fennarius left Paris in 1507, Vitoria must have taken his theology classes with him before that date. He studied liberal arts and theology with Crockart from 1509 to 1512. Crockart's high appreciation for the work of St. Thomas Aquinas is reflected in the works of Vitoria, who also considered Aquinas's ideas as the fundamental basis for metaphysical and philosophical theories.

In 1512, Vitoria's fruitful life as a student at the Sorbonne came to an end. He switched roles and became professor, albeit gradually. He taught liberal arts as a lecturer from 1512 to 1516 and then became professor of theology. Between liberal arts and theology, theology held the higher esteem at that time. Learning or teaching the arts was seen as a step toward achieving a fuller understanding of theology, since through art one could learn to philosophize about theology. It was also a general rule of the Dominican school that no one could teach theology without first having taught philosophy. This upward movement in Vitoria's teaching career began when Vitoria published Crockart's work, the *Secunda Secundae*, and a prologue to it in 1515. In 1522, he received his official licentiate in theology. Although he was highly acclaimed in Paris for his ingenuity and impressive skills as a professor, and finding a teaching position there would have been no problem at all, he returned to Spain shortly after receiving his licentiate and in 1523 was appointed *lector mayor* (senior lecturer) at Saint Gregory's in Valladolid, where he taught courses from 1523 to 1526.

In the summer of 1526, the *catedrático* (professor) of the University of Salamanca, Fray Pedro de León, died and the prestigious position of *prima chair* (first chair)[2] was left vacant. This position was very coveted and one needed extraordinary qualifications to be considered a candidate for it. The method and procedure for choosing a candidate was at the same time a popular and serious event. There was not the usual presence of an "official" tribunal to assess the virtues or downfalls of each candidate and make a selection. The students themselves were the judges. Although this was an unorthodox voting system that was not as easy to manage, it made more sense, since the students were the ones who knew the professors best and had firsthand experience with them. The students were also the ones who had the most to gain or lose from picking a qualified or unqualified candidate since their own future was at stake. This system also helped avoid creating a tribunal that would favor one opponent over another for reasons other than their scholarly virtues. This type of "universal suffrage" was limited only to university proceedings and legislation during this time. It also favored senior students, because each student was given the same number of votes as classes taken.

At first, Professor Diego de Astudillo seemed to be the most obvious choice for the position. However, although Astudillo had an impressionable well of knowledge to his disposal, he was still no match for Vitoria, who ended up being the unanimous choice of the students to replace Pablo de León. As Scott describes, "It is no slight tribute to democracy that a small, democratic, intellectual group should have chosen from among the intellectuals the one person best able to defend democracy for the entire world" (Scott 2000, 73).

1.1 VITORIA'S TEACHING

Vitoria never published any works of his own. The dates posted after the title of his *relecciones* in this work refer to the dates of his oral presentations. He gave lectures on aspects related to the New World and unfortunately, the only record we have of these come from his students' notes.[3] Vitoria introduced in Spain the slow-dictation style that was at a suitable pace for copying. The professor of theology at the University of Salamanca was required to give a public reading during the academic year and these were called *relectios*, a rereading of courses that had already taken place. Vitoria always gave lectures that were relevant to the political and cultural conditions of his day. For him, theology was the mother of all sciences and nothing could be fully understood without reference to theology, since it encompassed everything governed by divine and natural law. He believed that all matters concerning law must be based on philosophy and theology, which is why many scholars have named him one of the fathers of the philosophy of law. These lectures were demonstrative, not meant to debate the veracity of an argument but to explain it, which he did by skillfully manipulating the language to suit his own ideas.

One of the reasons for Vitoria's popularity as a professor of theology was this unique style of teaching. He presented his ideas in an eloquent fashion and very differently from the dry dictation method of teaching that was the prominent style in those days by adding flair with his language and taking great care and precision in preparing his lectures. A good witness of Vitoria's skills and influence as a professor was the enthusiasm of his students, who were said to see in Vitoria's teaching a real revival of theological learning in Spain. Melchor Cano, brothers Domingo and Pedro de Soto, Diego de Covarrubias, Domingo de Bañez, Domingo de Salazar, and Alonso de Veracruz, just to name a few, were among the students of Vitoria who were strongly influenced by his philosophical concepts and would soon achieve fame of their own following similar principles. Many of Vitoria's students became missionaries in the Indies and through their valuable eyewitness accounts he was able to remain well-informed and up-to-date on what was taking place in the New World.

The thorough, intense way in which Vitoria delivered his argument followed the basic methodology of Saint Tomas de Aquinas's *Summa Theologiae*: to discuss the opponents' case thoroughly, analyze each one of their conclusions and supporting arguments, to the point where one is almost convinced of the opponents' point of view, and then come around full force with reasons why their arguments could not be right according to this or that fundamental principle. Vitoria's passion for intellectual probing was clear in his teaching style as well. He was an indefatigable seeker of the truth, the "universal truth," which is why he did not study things from a single perspective but from a broader horizon and from different angles. He did this to fit his answers and solutions into a more universal conception.

Vitoria always had much faith in his authoritative sources and his most frequent references were to the past, a past that no longer existed. Two of the most cited authors in Vitoria's works are St. Thomas Aquinas and Aristotle. He also used sources such as the *Instituta* and *Digestum* of Justinian[4] and referred to the Bible when these contradicted the Vitorian concept of human rights, natural law, and justice. An interesting point is that while Vitoria makes abundant use of these authoritative sources as references for theological or legal issues, he relies entirely on his own authority in matters of morality.

Not everyone in Spain was delighted with Vitoria's arguments. This, however, did not really have any serious repercussions for him. The aforementioned readings of Vitoria, *De Indis* and *De Jure Belli*, in which he states, with no reservations, that the powers of the emperor and pope are limited, were delivered as public lectures and came to the attention of King Charles V. In November 1539, Charles V wrote a complaint addressed to the prior of the Dominican Convent of San Esteban in Salamanca, who happened to be Domingo de Soto at the time and who agreed with Vitoria's ideas and was destined to succeed him as professor of theology at the University of Salamanca. Charles V complained about the excessive liberty taken by Vitoria in discussing problems affecting the empire. Although this complaint was serious, it really had no effect on the teachings of Vitoria and he continued to exercise the same influence and authority in matters concerning the New World. This is illustrated especially by the fact that following the complaint, in 1541, Charles V wrote a letter speaking highly of the theologians of Salamanca and asking Vitoria for his advice on the instruction required by the Catholic faith for baptism, specifically with regard to the practice of forced baptism taking place in the Americas and whether or not this was justifiable and productive. The complaint also did not get in the way of Vitoria being invited by Charles V's son and successor, Phillip II, to attend the Council of Trent in 1545.

Vitoria became ill and was therefore unable to attend, but his disciple, Domingo de Soto, took his place. His health had deteriorated so much so that he became completely immobile and needed to be carried around. He had become "manco, tullido, inmóvil, con sólo la lengua expedita y sólo la cabeza sana" (In Getino 1930, 119). In other words, while Vitoria's physical disability deteriorated his body and rendered him helpless, his mind seemed to be as sharp as ever.

Vitoria's relationship with the Spanish Crown did not only pertain to the events following the complaint of Charles V. He had also been previously consulted by the Crown on other matters, one of which concerned the validity of the arguments of Henry VIII of England to annul his marriage to Charles's aunt, Catherine of Aragon, and the others regarding the treatment of the Amerindians in the New World. Also, very characteristic of Vitoria's independence and strong will was a complaint that he issued from his near-death bed in September 1543 about the marriage of Prince Phillip to the princess of Portugal. Vitoria did not agree with the extravagant way in which the wedding was being celebrated: "yo no veo título por donde, en buena conciencia, se pueda hacer tan gran gasto, que, a lo que entiendo, llegará a dos mil ducados . . . ¡parescerá que tenemos los doblones atesorados y no sabemos qué hacer con ellos!" (I do not see how, in good conscience, such a large cost can be made, which, I believe, will be as high as two thousand ducados.....it is going to seem as if we have currency stocked up and do not know what to do with it!) (In Getino 1936, 118).

As mentioned before, due to the fact that Vitoria had never officially published anything, we can only assume that the notes written down by his students were accurate. Vitoria's *relectios* were first published in 1557, with the first modern edition appearing in 1933. The *relectios* that will be the focus of this work and are considered by many scholars as fundamental texts of international law are *De Indis recenter invenitur relectio prior*, delivered as a lecture in 1538, and *De Indis sive de iure belli Hispanorum in barbaros relectio superior*, delivered in 1539.

Vitoria's intellectual development in Paris exposed him firsthand to the scholarly movement that was revolutionizing his political and cultural environment. Although St. Thomas de Aquinas seems to be one of the figures who made the deepest intellectual impact on Vitoria, it was Vitoria's stay in Paris that acquainted him with prominent humanists of the sixteenth century, such as Erasmus of Rotterdam and Juan Luis Vives, whose ideas and works also greatly influenced Vitoria's idea on the human being's place and natural rights in the world.

1.2 ERASMUS

Some scholars, such as Marcel Bataillon and James Scott, describe the feeling of Vitoria toward Erasmus as respectful, stating that even during the trial for Erasmus's potential heresy in his writings, Vitoria defended him, maybe not entirely his policies or his way of expressing them, but definitely his honor and dignity, out of respect for the man. Other intellectuals, such as Anthony Pagden, argue that "Vitoria's attitude towards the 'new grammarians,' as he called the humanists, hardened as the struggle against Lutheranism intensified, and he came to regard humanist textual scholarship on the Bible as the slippery slope which led to Protestant heresy" and that he believed that Erasmus should not be meddling in affairs that he did not understand (In Pagden 1991, xiv). Regardless, Desiderio Erasmus of Rotterdam did influence Vitoria's more progressive ideas and is one of the most well-known and discussed philosophers and theologians of the sixteenth century. Similar to Vitoria and Aquinas, he represented the struggle against tradition from within tradition itself and raised interesting questions from unique and different perspectives. During the early mid-sixteenth century, the "humanistic" and "reformistic" policies of the Dutch scholar Erasmus enjoyed great popularity among Spanish intellectuals. While at the Sorbonne in Paris the value of Erasmian texts were being debated, a Castilian theological conference at Valladolid upheld and defended them. Spain at that time could be considered an important center of European Erasmianism, particularly between 1527 and 1532, when Erasmian humanists were the chief religious advisers of the

Crown. The radicalization, polarization, and superstition of religious faiths in Europe during the mid-sixteenth century led to a hostile reaction against religions that were not Catholic in Castile and to an erosion of the influence of Erasmian counselors such as Juan and Alfonso de Valdés.[5] The suspicions ended up becoming so overwhelming and powerful that Erasmian doctrines began to be repressed under the oppressive weight of the Inquisition.

Erasmus was completely against the idea of imperial expansion with one ruler having complete control. Even though he was Charles V's adviser, he favored more peace among the Christian princes rather than Charles V's dream of universal hegemony, as the famous sonnet by Hernando de Acuña defines, "un monarca, un imperio, y una espada," (One monarch, one empire, and one sword) which he believed would only be an obstacle for that desired harmony. Erasmus was also an advocate of religious tolerance, which was what eventually led to the suspicions raised about him. He believed it would be more harmful to try and expatriate the heretics that lived among the Christians than just deal with the situation as it was: "Hay que tolerar a los malos mezclados con los buenos, puesto que había más daño en suprimirlos que en soportarlos" (One has to tolerate the bad converts together with the good ones, for it would be more damaging to eliminate them than to tolerate them.) (In Bataillon 1997, 261). At this time, religious tension in Spain was especially high because of the threat of Lutheran heresy to the Christian Church, and Erasmus's tolerance was what caused him to be suspicious in the eyes of church leaders and theologians, who saw it as promoting religious differences, even though this was not exactly the case. Erasmus argued that true religion was a matter of inward devotion rather than displays of church ceremonies and rituals. This concept laid the groundwork for Luther and his ideas. Luther borrowed in a sense the individualism of the humanists, the idea that each man could be his own priest and his body and mind was his church. The only real authority was the Bible, not the priests. This intensified the debate on the power and authority of the pope and its limitations. The main factor that separated Lutheranism from Erasmian humanism was Luther's idea that humans were incapable of following good for good's sake, whereas Erasmus displayed more optimism in the human race.

In 1527, Vitoria participated in a meeting in Valladolid called forth by the *Inquisidor General* (Great Inquisitor), Alonso Manrique, an Erasmus supporter himself, to analyze and discuss the potential risk of heresy in Erasmus's *Enchiridion militis Christiani*.[6] The Cortes was brought together in the summer of 1527, to discuss Erasmus's teachings. Vitoria was very careful in analyzing Erasmus's position and came to the conclusion that his stand on peace, and in particular his idea that tolerating heretic opinions was less harmful than destroying the peace of the church in order to go against them, could in fact lead to dangerous interpretations by some of his readers.

Erasmus himself did not want there to be anything that could be seen as going against the Christian religion in his writings. He agreed to write to the clergymen explaining his position in order to erase any doubts that his writings may have caused. These meetings never achieved a conclusion, since the proceedings were interrupted by an outbreak of the plague and never reconvened.

1.3 JUAN LUIS VIVES

Erasmus's most important disciple was the Valencian convert Joan Lluís Vives i March, or Juan Luis Vives (y March) as he was better known. Vives had witnessed the execution of several members of his immediate and wider family as Judaizers at the order of the Inquisition. His mother had been acquitted, but died of plague when Vives was only fifteen years old. After this, he left Spain never to return. This was not entirely due to the fact that he was a convert but also because he was attracted to Paris being the center of knowledge of the time. He studied in Paris for several years (1509–1512) and later moved to Belgium, where he became a professor of humanities at the University of Leuven in 1519. In association with Erasmus, he prepared a very detailed commentary on St. Augustine's *De Civitate Dei*, which was published in 1522. Soon after that he was invited to England as a tutor to Princess Mary (later Queen Mary I) and also wrote *De ratione estudii puerili sepisto la eduae* and *De institutione feminae Christianae*, on the education of women. While in England, he was made a doctor of law and lectured on philosophy at Corpus Christi College in Oxford. He was outspoken against the king's divorce from Catherine of Aragon, lost royal favor soon thereafter, and was placed on "house arrest" for about six weeks. When he was released, he went to Bruges, where he devoted the remainder of his life to composing numerous works such as *De Causis Corruptarum Artium*, which was mainly directed against scholastic philosophy and the unquestioning dominance and authority of Aristotle's theories.

Vives's criticism of inflexible scholastic logic came from his own personal experience in Paris, which was why, as he himself explained, no one could accuse him of condemning something that he had not fully experienced first-hand. He rejected the use of technical jargon claiming that it was useless, because it was only accessible to a limited audience. Describing things by using ambiguous phrases and explanations was ridiculous and inefficient. The need for an ordinary discourse to get a point across legibly rather than using the abstract language of the dialecticians was undeniable.

Vives was also extremely critical of the religious situation of the Spanish Empire. He paints a very somber picture of the deep divisions among Christians in his work, *De Europae dissidiis et bello Turcico*. He blamed the papacy for the massacres that had been taking place since the formation of the Liga de Cognac, made up of the enemies of the emperor in an attempt by the pope to gather support for his Italian ambitions that went against the wishes of Charles V.[7] Only peace among Christians would be enough to stop the advance of the Turks. Contrary to Erasmus and Vitoria, however, Vives believed that the emperor was an instrument of divine rule and that only under him peace and unification among the Christians could be achieved.

These outside influences and especially the impact of living, studying, and working in a city as intellectually vibrant as Paris are clearly illustrated in Vitoria's "liberal" ideas (liberal for the time in which they were written) in his *relectios* on the rights of the American Indians and human nature in general, the law of war, and the law of nations, all of which were based on the idea of a "common humanity" not only underlying but even dominating them. He returned to Spain as a citizen of the world, an internationalist, one who is aware that other countries exist beyond his own frontiers and wants to recognize and understand them as well as his own.

Vitoria, like Vives and Erasmus, believed strongly in the spiritual responsibility of human beings for one another, a responsibility that had no geographical limits. Vitoria's optimistic, and at times over-idealistic, outlook on the human race is clearly illustrated in his metaphysical discussions on the humanity inherent in all men and in their inclination toward the good. According to Vitoria, this was because God had created man to strive for the good, even though original sin had proved that man was vulnerable when it came to temptation. It was evident that God would never have created man with an inclination toward evil. This idealistic vision is reflected again in Vitoria's willingness to accept the "pagans" as equal to the Europeans, masters of themselves and of their possessions. He considered law and morality so intertwined that they should never, and could never, be separated.

Before discussing Vitoria's intellectual life in Salamanca in more detail, it is important to mention the Dominican Order to which a large part of his life was devoted and where many of his ideas began to take shape.

1.4 THE DOMINICAN ORDER AND ST. THOMAS AQUINAS

For the Dominican Order the primary theological text was St. Thomas Aquinas's *Summa Theologiae*, an encyclopedic synthesis of Christian doctrine and Aristotelian philosophy. Peter Crockart, under whom Vitoria studied philosophy and theology, was the first to replace the theological focus on Lombard's *Sententiae* with Aquinas's *Summa Theologiae*, an act which Vitoria considered very praiseworthy.[8]

St. Thomas Aquinas was born in the province of Aquino in Italy in 1225. His father was Landulph, count of Aquino, and his mother, Theodora, countess of Teano. Around the age of five, Thomas was sent to study under the Benedictine monks of Monte Cassino. In 1236, he was sent to another location to study, the University of Naples. Sometime between 1240 and 1243, he was received into the Order of St. Dominic. In 1244, Thomas was sent to Cologne to study under Albertus Magnus, an erudite theologian. In 1245, Albert was sent to Paris, and Thomas, his ardent disciple, accompanied him. In 1248, both returned to Cologne. Albert acquired the position of regent of the Dominican order, and Thomas became his teaching assistant. In 1252, Thomas officially took the position of Bachelor, or sub-regent, in the Dominican order in Paris. His teaching soon began to attract the attention of both professors and students. He mainly covered the *Sentences* of Peter Lombard, and his commentaries on that work laid down the foundation for his future claim to fame, the *Summa Theologiae*. Thomas received his degree of Doctor in Theology from the University of Paris in 1257. In 1259, he worked with his academic mentor Albert and with Peter of Tarentasia, who would later become Pope Innocent V, on constructing a generalized system of studies for the Dominican Order. On March 7, 1274, Thomas died and he was canonized in 1323 by Pope John XXII. We can see from this brief outline of St. Thomas's philosophical journey through life that he moved around frequently and was sent to many different places: Paris, Rome, Naples, Orvieto, Bologna, Cologne, and so on. The appreciation for his works had much to do with his clear ideas and the accuracy with which he delivered them. St. Thomas was driven by a very strong passion to explain, and sometimes even defend, the absolute "Christian truth."

St. Thomas published several works in his day, but by far the work that solidified his eminence in the circles of scholastic theology and beyond was his *Summa Theologiae*. This work was essentially a manual or scientific summary of the Christian doctrine originally intended for the use of students, but appealed to a larger audience due to its popularity. In the prologue to his work, St. Thomas criticized the lack of a scientific order in Christian philosophy, which led to confusion among students of the Christian doctrine. With the *Summa*, he attempted to systematize theology and make the Christian doctrine more understandable and therefore more accessible to students. He believed that using reason to explain the "Christian truth" was the best service one could give to God. However, he did not claim to have all the answers and he believed that philosophy did not consist so much in learning an established canon, but rather in finding out the truth. For Aquinas, natural law is the law of reason by which all human beings are led instinctively and is what ultimately determines the legitimacy of any human laws. Influenced by Gaius, Aquinas considered *ius gentium* (the law of nations) as a function of instinctive reason and therefore part of natural law. One can see the influence of Ulpian when he goes as far as stating that natural law is common to all animals as well and not solely to human beings.

Vitoria's style of writing was very similar to that of St. Thomas. They both possessed the ability to sift through already established ideas and use from them the points that would work best in solidifying their own perspective on a particular issue. This power of synthesis helped both of them fuse traditional ideas with newer ones. Their use and preference of sources was also very similar. The works that St. Thomas used most in his work and the ones for which he had the most respect were the Bible; works by the fathers of the church, especially St. Augustine;[9] the *Sentences* of Peter Lombard; and the works of important classical philosophers such as Plato and Aristotle. St. Thomas also used the ideas of Averroes, with whom he contended and argued in order to bring to light the "true" Aristotle.

Averroes believed that philosophy and religion belonged in two different spheres. Religion was more for the masses, many unlearned, whereas philosophy was more specifically for the chosen, the learned, the few. Philosophy and religion were on completely distinct levels. However, nothing in a true religious belief could be opposed to reason because if so, then religious belief in itself would be false. Philosophy could neither be irreligious nor oppose religious principles, since these were not simply absurd ideas without a foundation. Averroes saw this concept illustrated perfectly by Aristotle. St. Thomas, on the other hand, believed in addressing these "false interpretations" of Aristotle in order to uncover the "true Aristotelian" argument and apply it to Christian teachings with no contradictions. Here St. Thomas echoes his *maestro*, St. Albertus Magnus, who in turn follows St. Augustine's idea, that whatever truth there was in the works of the "pagan" philosophers should be extracted from their writings and adapted to the Christian doctrine.

St. Thomas's "rehabilitation" of Aristotle's ideas in order to fit his own agenda is again very similar to the way Vitoria manipulates the pagan philosopher's ideas to blend in with his own. Aristotle's conception of natural slaves is a perfect example of an Aristotelian idea directly contradicting Vitoria's idea that natural law was applicable to all human beings equally. As Scott explains, "The fact of the matter appears to be that Aristotle was in fact guilty of the charge of denying natural rights, and it was only by an interpretation of what Vitoria thought Aristotle had meant rather than what he said, that the 'pagan saint' was not stricken from his calendar" (Scott 2000, 114). Vitoria argued that Aristotle in his theory on natural slaves meant to say that there existed people of "feeble mind" that for their own good and well-being should be governed by others more intelligent and apt until they (the "feeble-minded") learned by their (the more intelligent) example and could govern themselves. This idea was very similar to the conception that was gaining popularity at the time, of the American Indians as children, in need of education and "humanization" by the more learned and civilized, until they came of age so to speak and could independently manage their own affairs "correctly," which meant more like the Spanish of course.

The *Summa* contains 38 treatises and 612 questions, which are subdivided into 3,120 seperate categories, and in which 10,000 objections are addressed. It took St. Thomas about eight years to compose his work, which he started in Rome in 1265 and "finished" in Naples in 1272.[10] The *Summa* ended up replacing the *Sentences* as the primary textbook for theologian studies.

St. Thomas believed that the Aristotelian system of analysis was the most powerful and complete system of thought available, and his own systemization of philosophical ideas came from his conviction of the veracity of Aristotle's arguments. Aristotle was one of the first philosophers to make philosophy coexist with science and attempted to make logic a science as well. For Aristotle, experience, or firsthand revelation, was the true source of knowledge. Without witnessing things firsthand, one could not find out the "real truth." Things are only made entirely intelligible and understandable through the processes of active intellect.

Aquinas is thought of as the main catalyst behind the shift of the focus in scholastic theology from Plato to Aristotle. Aquinas created a new philosophical ideology which combined fundamentals of Christian teaching with elements of Aristotelian philosophy. Although he achieved a very high level of popularity, many ecclesiastical authorities and theologians did not agree with Aquinas. As a matter of fact, some of Aquinas's ideas were officially condemned in 1277 by leading churchmen in Paris. The Dominicans, on the other hand, with a strong sense of loyalty to one of their forbearers, stood solidly behind the ideas and works of Aquinas and officially took up the defense of his work in 1286, making it the official philosophy to be taught at their colleges. Vitoria, being an ardent disciple of St. Thomas, followed his Aristotelian-based ideas as well. Scholar Annabel Brett points out Vitoria's tendency to bend and shape Thomist teaching to fit into concepts and answer questions that had not been addressed by St. Thomas himself and to address the new problems of the sixteenth century in her extensive work on the history of natural law and rights, *The Oxford Handbook of the History of International Law*, as well as in *Changes of State: Nature and the Limits of the City in Early Modern Natural Law*, where she describes it as the "reconstitution" and "redeployment" of Aquinas's theory of natural law.

An interesting aspect of the Dominican Order that must have played a part in influencing Vitoria's ideas was its internal structure. The Order resembled a representative democracy, with the officers elected by representative bodies. In this sense, the Dominican Order could be seen as a model, a forerunner, of the future form of representative government. The Dominican Order's enormous influence made it a very significant force in Spanish society and in the decision-making process regarding the Americas. The New World for the Dominicans represented the perfect place for their work of spreading Christian religion by preaching the word of God. Of course, this was the vision of not only the Dominicans but of other religious orders as well, such as the Franciscans and the Jesuits. These three orders, different in many ways, were similar in their view of the Americas as virgin territory perfect for making the word of God known to the "innocents" who had never been introduced to the "real" faith. Dominican convents, such as Vitoria's San Pablo, often witnessed the arrival and departure of missionaries to and from the New World. This enabled Vitoria to hear firsthand accounts of the affairs of the colonies.

1.5 THEOLOGIANS AND THE SCHOOL OF SALAMANCA

Vitoria seemed to be involved in the American Indian question throughout his life. In Burgos, the place of his childhood, he was at the center of the dispute over American Indian rights, and Valladolid, where he held his first teaching position in Spain, became the seat of the Council of the Indies and was where the great debate between Bartolomé de Las Casas and Juan Ginés de Sepúlveda took place in 1550–1551 over the rights of the American Indians and Spain's right to colonize the already inhabited New World. It was also here that Vitoria began discussing in his lectures the issues of the indigenous people and their natural and human rights with regard to the Spanish conquest. As Brian Tierney describes, the Spanish encounter with America redirected the course of human rights thinking for the future and "stirred up the rights of Amerindians among Spanish scholars, especially Vitoria and Las Casas and on the other side, Sepúlveda. At that time an ideal of human rights was passionately asserted and vigourously contested" (Tierney 2004, 3).

Vitoria's teaching position in Valladolid gave him the opportunity to take a big part in the debate over the conquest of the Americas and analyze in his lectures the legitimate versus illegitimate titles of Spanish conquest and rights of the American Indians. It was under Vitoria and his admirable attempt to create a moral philosophy of law that would include classic Roman law texts within a new developing discourse centered on natural law and divine law that the University of Salamanca attained a renowned position of revived theological scholasticism.

The University of Salamanca was considered during the sixteenth century one of the greatest universities, not only in Spain, but worldwide. Its importance was actually already established in the twelfth century and its prominence lasted until the nineteenth century. Before Vitoria, the University of Salamanca had achieved its fame and outstanding reputation from its studies of civil and canon law, but in large part due to the debates and the emergence of a new, developing intellectual framework following the conquest of the New World, the University of Salamanca became the scene of a revival of theological scholarship. This newfound devotion to the question of the American Indian status and human rights in turn gave origin to a group of intellectuals known as the School of Salamanca, or the second scholastic, which refers to a group of theologians and intellectuals, not all Dominicans, that shared the same political and moral ideas. Francisco de Vitoria, Domingo de Soto, Martin de Azpilcueta, Tomás de Mercado, Luis de Molina, and Francisco Suárez were patrons, some founders, of this school/club of theologians and jurists that focused their thoughts and discussions on natural law and morality and embraced the challenge of combining the teaching of Aquinas with the new, emerging political-economic order and finding an effective harmonious relationship between the two. After the conquest of Peru with its horrific details, such as the bloody massacre of the Incan court and civil population at Cajamarca,[11] a majority of the intellectuals of the School of Salamanca began strongly denouncing the oppression that accompanied the first evangelization attempts in the Americas and questioning the until then unquestioned Spanish claims to legitimacy and dominion in the New World, deriving their arguments form natural law rather than divine law.

The first objective of School of Salamanca intellectuals such as Domingo de Soto and Vitoria was to teach the American Indians first how to become civilized human beings by living among the Spaniards and learning by example, thereby achieving their "humanization," while at the same time learning how to be proper Christians. The question of evangelization and the correct, morally just way to go about it had to do not only with the correct form of religious instruction but also, and many times more importantly, with the question of human rights. This is somewhat paradoxical, since to recognize individuals' human rights would imply granting them freedom of choice, of religion, and to be themselves. Notwithstanding, this perspective was successful in restructuring the traditional concept of natural law. The conclusion was that since human beings share the same nature, they also possess the same human rights: liberty and equality. This recognition of universal rights was a revolutionary break from the Aristotelian concept of natural slaves.

During the sixteenth century, especially between 1526 and 1546, many issues arose that were a direct or indirect result of the conquest of the Americas: international relations and emerging nation-states, the relationship between the latter and the church, the rights of the Spaniards in the New World, the lawfulness of preaching Christianity overseas, and so on. These factors only added to the tension that the traditional Roman Catholic concept of man and his place in the world in relation to God had already been experiencing, primarily due to the rise of the Protestant Reformation and humanism. The abovementioned theories of the majority of the scholars of the School of Salamanca only exasperated this situation.

These scholars also dismissed completely the idea that the pope and the church were the supreme political global authority and had control over the entire world. Rather, they argued that there were two realms of power, one in the natural or civil realm and one in the supernatural or spiritual realm. One immediate consequence of this theory was that it established that neither did the king or emperor have complete authority or jurisdiction over souls nor did the pope or the Catholic Church possess legitimate temporal power. This theory went directly against the dominant concept of the time which rested on the divine right of the king, the universal authority of the pope, and Alexander VI's bull of demarcation. This papal bull asserted that the Catholic faith should be praised, preached, and spread throughout the world to save the souls of those in barbarous nations, who had not yet heard the word of God, and teach them how to live a good, civilized, and God-fearing life.

Pope Alexander VI, the second pope from the Borja family and himself a Spaniard from Xativa, Valencia, granted the request on behalf of Spain to give them authority over most of the newly discovered lands in three bulls issued on May 3 and May 4, 1493. These bulls were overwhelmingly in favor of Spain, depriving Portugal of the privileges it had been given by Nicholas V's bulls of 1452 and 1454, Sixtus IV's bull of 1481, and Innocentius's bull of 1484. On September 26, 1493, a fourth bull was issued that gave Spain almost unlimited rights and authority over the new lands. However, this bull never fully took shape and to avoid complications that were already brewing, the Spanish Crown decided to hold a conference to reach an agreement. Ambassadors from Portugal went to Barcelona, and after a considerable amount of time negotiating, a settlement was reached between the two parties in Tordesillas on June 7, 1494. In the Treaty of Tordesillas, a line of separation was created that officially divided the newly discovered territories between Portugal and Spain, leaving most of the territories under the dominion of Spain but leaving what would become Brazil for Portugal. Although controversial and much disputed, the Treaty of Tordesillas remained in effect until January 13, 1750, when the Treaty of Madrid finally nullified the boundary line that had been set. Alexander VI's papal command marked the beginning of the colonization and conversion process in the New World.

A majority of the scholars of the School of Salamanca argued that societies were natural entities, there to protect the weak and vulnerable. Society was the only place where man could exercise his gifts of reason, judgment, and virtue. Since all societies were natural organisms, it logically followed that no individual could have had ruling power before the formation of the societies. Therefore, it was obvious that all the civil power rested first and foremost in the commonwealth. The commonwealth then transferred that power to a ruler. Even though the king did have power over the commonwealth, it did not go unchecked; he would have to answer to and obey the same laws as his subjects, and if he failed to do so he would be as guilty as any of them. People were the vehicle of divine sovereignty and they in turn passed this power (symbolically) to a king or an emperor under certain conditions. However, an aspect of Vitoria's argument in respect to this which is seemingly contradictory is when he states that kings and popes get royal power from God himself, thus creating a confusing distinction between divine sovereignty and royal power:

> It is apparent that even though sovereigns are set up by the commonwealth, royal power derives immediately from God. For example, the Pope is elected and crowned by the Church, but nevertheless papal power does not come from the Church but from God himself. In the same way, the power of sovereigns clearly comes immediately from God himself, even though kings are created by the commonwealth. (In Pagden 1991, 16)

Vitoria then "clarifies" this stating that "the commonwealth does not transfer to the sovereign its power, but simply its own authority; there is no question of two separate powers, one belonging to the sovereign and the other to the community" (In Pagden 1991, 16).

Vitoria assumed an ordered universe and adopted the Thomist hierarchy of laws: eternal law, which governed all things and was the reason of God to be recognized by all; law, already inscribed in the mind, innately existing within a person, and through which one distinguishes good from evil without the actual act of reasoning; divine law, which was the will of God; and human law (civil and canon law), which required the use of reasoning and was made by men in accordance, of course, with natural law.

The most fundamental change that Vitoria introduced was a redefinition of the grounds on which the Spanish Crown rested its authority in the New World. Instead of legitimizing Spanish sovereignty in the Americas through the heroic messianic concept used by the Spanish Crown, by Las Casas, and by conquistadores such as Cortés, Bernal Diaz, or Pizarro, the Spanish presence and domination in the New World was justified on a more secular and rational basis. More importance was now put on the power of the Spanish to introduce and create universal and just laws than their power as preachers and propagandists of the Christian faith.

The ultimate goal of the scholars of the School of Salamanca was the creation of a morally just colonial order and the right of the American Indians to self-govern, a relatively new concept for that time. This would be accomplished by a Christian, morally bound state, where morality would always be applied to politics. For the Salamanca intellectuals, politics were inseparable from ethics and there was a universal ethical code which should be acknowledged. Even though their plans for a successful, peaceful "colonial reconversion" did not succeed, the theories of the School of Salamanca introduced a humanitarian perspective that would, or at least attempted to, be followed up to our present day; "La Escuela de Salamanca definió las bases éticas y los presupuestos políticos para un proyecto de reconversión colonial . . . a pesar de sus éxitos y fracasos abrió nuevas vías de progresión jurídica y moral para el pensamiento del Occidente cristiano y de la humanidad entera" (The School of Salamanca defined the ethical and political bases for a project of colonial conversion... in spite of their successes and failures they opened new ways towards judicial and moral progress in Western Christian thinking and that of all humanity) (*Carta Magna de los indios* 1988, 7). As mentioned before, the reputation and authority that the University of Salamanca gained during the sixteenth century can be attributed in large part to the popularity and authority of Francisco de Vitoria, earned by his vast knowledge and perception of what was happening in the world at the time.

The Crown's "responsibility" for the evangelization of the American Indians made clergymen, who had always been important in royal councils, trusted advisers to the Crown and to the Council of the Indies on matters concerning the American Indians. In this sense, many clergymen and theologians in sixteenth-century Spain believed that their duties and responsibilities extended over such a vast field, that no argument, topic, or discussion seemed alien to them. This was where Francisco de Vitoria stepped in and commanded the stage. In discussing in a series of lectures the juridical and theological bases for Spanish sovereignty in the New World, he revolutionized the political, theological, philosophical, and cultural concepts of sixteenth-century Spanish society, the effects of which can still be seen today. As Luciano Pereña states,

> Vitoria formuló la hipótesis de la legitimidad de la permanencia de España en América . . . el maestro de Salamanca inició una verdadera revolución cultural y política. Fue mérito suyo haber provocado esta tensión . . . porque no se puede desconocer que en esta parte frenó el espíritu de aventura y paralizó la arrollada expansión militar de los ejércitos españoles. La autocrítica de la Escuela ha hecho posible un balance global. (Vitoria formulated the hypothetical legitimacy of Spain's permanent presence in America. . . the Salamanca scholar started a veritable cultural and political revolution. He was responsible for creating this tension. . . because one cannot ignore the fact that in this respect he halted the spirit of adventure and paralyzed the dynamic expansion of the Spanish armed forces. The self-criticism of the School of Salamanca has facilitated a global balance) (*Carta Magna de los indios* 1988, vii)

NOTES

1. This was the case with the many of the Iberian Jews in an attempt to hide their Jewish origins and escape persecution and discrimination. Examples here are Bartolomé de Medina and St. Thomas de Aquinas.

2. Scott explains the *prima* chair position more in detail; "In Salamanca there were two chairs, the *prima* and the *vespera*, indicating the hours of the day when a course should be given. That of the *prima* professor began at the prime hour, according to canonical custom, which was none other than six o'clock in the morning . . . the earlier the hour the greater the honour" (73).

3. Many of Vitoria's lectures were copied down by Domingo de Soto, and published in *De iustitia et iure*, an important text on justice and rights.

4. The "official" codification of Roman law was directed by the emperor Justinian, 527–565. The *Corpus Juris Civilis* was part of a compilation of sources into several parts: the *Codex*, a collection of law enactments from Imperial Rome that were repealed; the *Digest*, a lengthy summary of the teachings of important Roman jurists of the imperial period; the *Institutes*, which summarized and made accessible, and understandable for that matter, the law of the Roman Empire, a law which Justinian tried to revive during the sixth century; and the *Novellae*, which were several new laws that Justinian had promulgated in following years. He was unsuccessful at these attempts and it was not until the eleventh century that this Roman law tradition was reinstated and formed the basis for the law system found in most European countries.

5. These twin brothers were loyal followers of Erasmus's teachings. Both were against the abuse of power by the church and the pope, especially after the sack of Rome in 1527. Alfonso's work, *Diálogo de Lactancio*, directly addressing this "catastrophe" and vindicating the emperor, and Juan's work, *Diálogo de Mercurio y Canon*, with a more religious dialogue mixed in with the political one, were published together in *Lactancio* in 1529.

6. Vitoria attended four juntas: on July 2, 8, and 22 and on August 6. He was a very influential person at that time and his opinion was held in very high regard: "esa influencia extraordinaria atribuída a Vitoria por Erasmo, por sus amigos, por el Inquisidor que le consultaba especialmente y le mandaba la primera de las citaciones; esa influencia, bien extraña en quien llevaba sólo un año en Salamanca, no pudo manifestarse por la disolución de la Junta" (That extraordinary influence attributed to Vitoria by Erasmus, by his friends, and by the Inquisitor who especially sought his advice and sent him the first of the summons; that influence, unusual for someone who had only been one year in Salamanca, was unable to manifest itself due to the dissolution of the Junta) (Getino 1930, 105).

7. These enemies of Emperor Charles V included the king of France, Francis I, and the Italian dukes of Milan, Florence, and Venice.

8. The *Sentences*, or *Quatuor libri Sententiarum*, is the theological discourse that gave fame to Peter Lombard, its author, written around 1150. The work is divided into four books and systematically addresses a whole series of questions on the

Christian theological doctrine. He summarizes traditional Christian doctrines and the different opinions surrounding each one at the time. Lombard's work is primarily a compilation of previous texts from different sources. The author makes no attempt to hide this; his idea had been to create a collection of various important arguments on the Christian doctrine and put them all together in one work, thereby saving the trouble of looking up different sources and making it more accessible to a larger audience.

9. St. Augustine is well-known for his work, *Civitae Dei, The City of God.* When Rome's overarching imperial unity fell and its imperfections were realized, many of the Christian faith were worried about the stability of the Christian religion. Augustine developed the idea of the church as a spiritual city of God, completely separate from the material city of man that helped put these worries at ease as well as strengthen the idea of papal supremacy.

10. St. Thomas never actually finished the *Summa*, he went up to the ninetieth question in the section On Penance in the third part of his work.

11. Pizarro and team of a little over 100 foot soldiers and 60 or so horsemen arrived at Cajamarca and demanded to see and speak to Atahualpa. Pizarro sent Hernando de Soto, friar Vicente de Valverde, and native interpreter Felipillo to approach Atahualpa. Atahualpa, however, refused to acknowledge the Spanish conquistador's demands. His refusal led Pizarro and his force to attack the Incan army in what became the Battle of Cajamarca on November 16, 1532. The Spanish were successful despite being drastically outnumbered and created one of the biggest massacres in Latin American history.

Chapter 2

Vitoria and Law

In order to be able to understand Vitoria's concept of human rights, *bellum justum* (just war), and jus gentium (law of nations), it is essential to study first his overall ideas on law, its hierarchy, the powers allotted to each aspect of it, his concept of the state, and his view on the church. In his opinion, law and morality were so intertwined that they should never, and could never, be separated. *Jus* was what was just, the just act itself. Justice stemmed from *jus* and not the other way around. Vitoria's view on justice and natural law is in accordance with the theory posited by St. Thomas Aquinas in his *Summa Teológica*, namely that all rights are natural and the result of God's law, not of His grace. The essence of law for Vitoria, as well as for Aquinas, was that it ultimately belonged to the will and reason of God. Quoting Aquinas, Vitoria described it as "nothing but a dictate of practical reason which God has possessed from eternity" (In Pagden 1991, 1163). Aquinas states that natural law is a set of self-evident principles given to us by God at our creation. It consists of two parts: the first being the primary principles that no human can fail to realize, since they are already intrinsic in the mind, and second being the secondary principles, which are the conclusions drawn rationally from the first principles and applied to law. As Tung describes, "According to Aquinas and Vitoria, mankind has two ends, natural (*felicitas politica*) and supernatural happiness (*ultima felicitas*). Mankind's two ends dictate the bivalent sovereign order of the secular commonwealths and the Roman Church. Princes 'deal with human happiness' while pontiffs attend to 'supernatural felicity'" (Tung 2012, 10).

For Vitoria the fundamental notion behind natural law and law in general was that nature was God's creation and the human conscience had to answer to God. This was what, for him, made theology a universal science. From this point, Vitoria embarked on a theological mission to develop a discipline from which no human being was exempt, an omnipresent concept of theology. This objective would be hard to obtain however because, as Brian Tierney effectively points out, there cannot be one set of natural and human rights valid for the hundreds of societies in the world with their different values, customs, and traditions, since "peoples are irremediably molded in different ways by their different cultures" (Tierney 2004, 3).

2.1 DIVINE LAW

In Spain, the one thing on which most intellectuals agreed was that all human laws had to abide by and follow divine law and natural law. Vitoria preached the idea of uniting mankind not just by juridical institutions but also by the concept of a universal humanity where man had to answer not only to law but also to his responsibility and especially guilt with respect to his fellow man. In part, this fusion was already accomplished after the Roman Empire became Christian under Constantine, but gathered much more force under Justinian, when the idea of Christian salvation was added to the Roman concept of law. Roman law had put a great deal of emphasis on man as a citizen, but not so much on the concept of man as a human being, an idea which Christianity articulates at a later date. Christian theory used natural law and divine law as links between ethics and morality, and legal and political theories, links which helped establish the Vitorian doctrines of just war and international law and also another way in which the church was able to control the people.

Divine morals were handed down from God directly and natural law was defined by man's rationalization. In Thomistic thought, divine law was the kind of law residing in God with power over all things inclining mankind toward the good. Man is guided by God through his own reason and will to his intended end. Aristotle described this law as perfect and infinite, an example of human dominion. The power and freedom with which mankind is endowed in divine law are transferred through participation in eternal law: "To participate in the Eternal law, hence, is to be cognizant of the natural ordering of things according to Divine will" (Valenzuela-Vermehren 2013, 85). Power comes from God but ultimately pertains to the community.

For scholars and theologians of fifteenth- and sixteenth-century Spain, according to divine law the pope exercised universal jurisdiction in order to accomplish the divine mission of spreading Christianity. It was under this notion that Pope Alexander VI's papal bull divided the newly conquered territories between the Portuguese and the Spanish colonizers. The powers granted to the Spaniards in this bull were not only unlimited but overarching as well, since they gave them authority over pretty much everything that they encountered in the New World. Rulers latched onto this concept and more often than not used it to suit their own purposes. They proceeded to invade "infidel" territory, relying on the pope's authority to legitimize such conquests. This was done, for example, during Pizarro's conquest of Peru in 1536, with all of its horrific details, and during the conquest of Tenochtitlán by Cortez, who manipulated this messianic concept to suit his own goals. Therefore, through violent military conquest, these rulers were carrying out the pope's jurisdiction that he really possessed only in theory.

Vitoria's reaction to the atrocities committed in the Americas in the mid-sixteenth century caused him to argue strongly against these practices and in doing so, he ended up replacing the conventional basis for Spanish sovereignty in the New World, the divine law of the pope, with universal natural law, or the law system of jus gentium, the rules of which may be ascertained by the use of reason. This actually gave King Charles V more freedom from the pope's absolute power, while making the humanity of the American Indians a requirement needed to fully legitimize the theory of natural law and its supreme power. However, these two types of law were not mutually exclusive, but rather they worked together, as Vitoria describes, "Nothing which is permitted in natural law is prohibited in the gospels" (In Pagden 1991, 15). Divine law, like natural law, was unalterable and could not be modified by man. In both laws, the greatest sin one could commit was to offend the honor of God or that of one's neighbor.

2.2 NATURAL LAW

Since natural law is universal and perpetual and therefore has validity everywhere, it is always binding, so there is no need to wait for its promulgation before it becomes official. According to early philosophers such as Socrates, Plato, and Aristotle, humans lived in a rational and morally directed universe and the moral order of the world was already inherent in them since the day of creation. Aristotle is the most well-known philosopher for his advocacy of natural law. In *Rhetoric*, he argued that aside from particular laws that people and communities have set up for themselves, there existed a common, universal law that was right according to nature. Laws could vary from place to place, but what was real by nature was the same everywhere. This philosophy, to live according to nature, was also the core ideology on which Stoicism was based.

Stoicism was founded by Zeno circa 336 B.C. His first written work, *Commonwealth*, became the primary text for the Stoic school. Zeno argued that a commonwealth was one perfect state that included the whole world. There would be no citizens of different states but rather citizens of the world. There would be no courts, since this "perfect state" would anger no one and virtue would be the supreme force with love as its guiding light. Only the law of nature would apply in this idealistic state; no law "tainted" by man would work. Since universalism and reason existed in the community from the very beginning, no additional laws needed to be made. The strength and popularity of Stoic philosophy rested primarily on its powerful belief in the foundation of natural equity. Stoic philosophy also maintained that there was a rational order to the universe, directed toward the purpose of well-being, and the way a human being lived according to this order was under natural law, which essentially dictated virtuous acts. All laws were to be evaluated and judged by their conformity to natural law. Everything that happened in this world had its destined place within a larger rational order. Stoic philosophy regarded the universe as having a purposeful order that was governed by divine or eternal law, and the way in which individuals or societies lived in accordance with this structured order of the universe was natural law. In Stoic philosophy, natural law focused on the morality of actions taken rather than their possible consequences. Due to this, the fundamental basis of natural law was determined by whatever constituted true happiness. For example, state bound by natural law had as its ultimate objective the happiness of its people.

In Greek philosophy, nature consisted of the physical, visible aspects of the universe and in time this concept was extended to the thoughts and soul of man. With this expansion, the Greek law of nature created a system of simple rules by which to organize and resolve the moral dilemmas of society. Ironically enough, in spite of the pagan elements in this natural law theory, many of the early Christian Church priests wanted to incorporate it into Christian teachings. During the sixteenth century, Vitoria and his colleagues of the School of Salamanca further developed the theory of Christian natural law.

For Vitoria natural law was the omnipresent force of the world, the law of the universe. It governed everything that had to do with society. When speaking of this type of law, it is important to keep in mind that it arose as a response to the question of whether or not mankind could live without law of any kind. In Christian natural law theory, theoretical questions such as the nature of God and the dual nature of Christ were the most important. One may be tempted to question why God, the Creator, would not let his people live and do as they pleased, since he had given them free will, *libre albedrío*, and instead bind them by rules. In Christian theory, the answer to this was that, although rules and laws may inhibit our free will as individuals, they were also necessary for our well-being. A society with no limits or restrictions would actually be harmful to its components, and rules were needed for safety from others as well as from oneself.

According to Christian natural law theory, the human being was given intellect and reason to make moral choices and to be able to recognize virtue and beauty in art and culture. For Vitoria, free reason was free will, to be the master of one's own actions. Since the human condition did not allow to do as one pleased or follow one's own impulses, while living in harmony with others, a standard was needed to which all human beings should model their acts. This is where natural law stepped in and became a moral law of conduct applicable to all.

As mentioned before, St. Thomas Aquinas described natural law as having two kinds of precepts: the most general ones, known to everyone everywhere, and the more detailed precepts, which are actually the conclusions of the first precepts. The general precepts can in no way be absent from any individual, since they are inherent in human nature. It is what enables humans to distinguish good from evil. However, the secondary precepts can fall victim to evil temptations, customs, or habits.

Vitoria makes a very interesting point that "natural law is not so called because it exists within us by nature: children have neither natural law nor the disposition of it within them. It is so called because we judge what is right by natural inclination, not because of some naturally implanted quality" (In Pagden 1991, 169). He maintained an optimistic outlook on human nature and believed that it was always inclined toward the good and never arose from the bad. A person cannot be inherently cruel because God would not create intrinsic evil: "A natural inclination cannot be towards evil, because it comes from God, as St. Thomas argues on the subject of the sin of the first angel, and the evil would then be imputed to God as the giver" (In Pagden 1991, 171). Vitoria was clearly in agreement neither with Aristotle's more pessimistic view on human nature of man nor with the Lutheran idea of the natural evil and corrupt nature of the human being.

There are problems with this optimistic ideology and how Vitoria addressed the incongruences. If people were by nature good, what made some seem inclined toward evil? Vitoria here explained that the inclination that seemed to be toward evil stemmed from the question of whether people were more inclined to the general good, the good for the community, or their individual good. The latter was the one with which Vitoria encountered the most difficulties with the rest of his argument on human nature. According to him, people's selfishness made them think first of their own individual good rather than focus on the good of the community, and this was what could easily lead one to succumb to evil temptations and become detrimental to society.

There were also those, such as Juan Ginés de Sepúlveda, who believed the Roman philosophy that there were two kinds of natural law, one common to both humans and animals, and one particular only to rational and civilized nations (implying that among the latter Spain's was the best). The civilized nations had the obligation of not only correctly interpreting natural law but also imposing it, if necessary by force, on "barbarians." Here we see the

Aristotelian idea that a "natural aristocracy" implied a "natural servitude." Vitoria did not agree and firmly believed that the inhabitants of the New World, and all pagans in general, had natural rights of their own, upon which no other "superior" civilization or religion could justifiably infringe.

According to Vitoria, natural law exists among all people, not only Christians. It is a natural system of ethics that neither contradict nor depended on Christian revelation. By natural law all men are born free, except for paternal and marital dominion of course. Since that was the case, Vitoria raised an important question in his *relectio*, *On Civil Power*: "Who then has the right to reduce man, thus created free, into servitude?" (In Pagden 1991, 13). This was to be a key point in the criticisms of Spanish colonial policy, because with this argument Vitoria concluded that the powers that a Christian prince received from God were not only given to Christian princes but under natural law were also found among "infidels" and pagan princes: "There can be no doubt at all that the heathens have legitimate rulers and masters. . . . So neither Christian sovereigns nor the church may deprive non-Christians of their kingship or power on the grounds of their unbelief" (In Pagden 1991, 18).

2.3 HUMAN LAW (POLITICAL COMMUNITY AND ITS LAWS)

Vitoria believed that natural law regulated the relationship of man with the world, and therefore governed every practice in human society. Human law, on the other hand, was a series of laws created by people with its ultimate purpose being social happiness. In order for these to be legitimate they had to derive from some aspect of natural law, on which everything was based. A Roman body of law was developed by the first century B.C. that applied equally to citizens and noncitizens and was different from the civil law that was specific to a particular state. Contrary to natural law, human law needed an official promulgation before it could become binding. Vitoria emphasized that it needed to be a public act of promulgation or else it was not official; a private promulgation among a select group of people was not enough, "it takes a solemn act of promulgation to make a law binding" (In Pagden 1991, 162). Human law came from God just as much as natural and divine law did, even though it came more indirectly through "men as agents of power":

> It is apparent that even though sovereigns are set up by the commonwealth, royal power derives immediately from God. For example, the pope is elected and crowned by the Church, but nevertheless papal power does not come from the Church, but from God himself. In the same way, the power of the sovereign clearly comes immediately from God himself, even though kings are created by

> the commonwealth. That is to say, the commonwealth does not transfer to the sovereign its power (*potestas*), but simply its own authority (*auctoritas*). (In Pagden 1991, 16)

The freedom of mankind to make laws was an inalienable power which, contrary to authority, could not be transferred to rulers. Human law was essential for a functional society because natural law was not sufficiently detailed. It always needed to be directed first and foremost to the common good of the people.

Vitoria was a proponent of the "new idea" of social life at this time, according to which the state and society were the most important things and the ruler's primary objective was to safeguard the well-being of the republic. In order to introduce this concept more smoothly into the Spanish political system, Vitoria found it best never to stray too far from tradition and to intertwine the new concepts he wished to introduce with the traditional ones that already existed. His position on issues would always stem from elements that in one way or another were already present in tradition but allowed him still to mold them to the new ideas that he wanted to incorporate. This was one of Vitoria's best skills: the ability to innovate within the traditional canon and bring to light new ideas out of established ones of the past. His innovation, which was primarily the separation of divine law and natural law, and the emphasis he placed on the power of the people, had a huge impact on theological and philosophical studies then and still now. The way in which he used the power of language and manipulated it to convince his readers and strengthen his argument was impressive.

In making a distinction between "power" and "authority," Vitoria made sure never to stray too far from the concept of civil power, or any power at all for that matter, being a gift from God. He did introduce some variations, however, by claiming that power was vested in the prince by God, but the authority to use such power must come from the community, because ultimately the communal body was the key to sovereignty, and not just the king. For this reason, a government with a king as head of state whose power derived from the people was the most efficient and just. This was a much different position from the one that Roman law had originally established of the ruler as free from the law and as sole source of law. For this reason, I disagree with political scholar Quentin Skinner's opinion that Vitoria's ideas can be associated with absolutist theory. Vitoria articulated the different kinds of regime that Aquinas defined: monarchy, where one man rules; aristocracy, where a few men rule; and democracy, where the people rule. Referring to Aristotle, Vitoria claimed that a monarchical government with a certain dose of the other systems was the greatest form of rule because it provided the cohesion necessary for a society's stability, which was especially evident during Charles V's reign over many different and vast territories.

It was necessary to achieve unification, not just of the vast territories of the kingdom but also within Spain itself, a Spain that was divided religiously, culturally, and socially, and in Vitoria's opinion only the king, the head of society, would be able to provide that cohesion. Vitoria used the authority of Aristotle and Aquinas in describing how of the three forms of government, monarchy, aristocracy, and democracy, monarchy was the best, because under one ruler there would be more union, more control, and less confusion. However, he then proceeded to criticize Aquinas's inconsistency in also stating that a mixed form of government was the best: "But on the other hand Aquinas is saying here that the best form of government is the mixed and he repeats this idea above in I-II. 95. 4. His opinions are therefore inconsistent" (In Pagden 1991, 198). This seems ironic, first of all considering the fact that Vitoria himself displayed this indecisive trait quite frequently, and second, because it was Vitoria's opinion that a king could only rule with the authority granted him by the people, which would make it a monarchy with a little bit of democracy mixed in. He believed that neither a king nor the people should have all the power and authority. He deemed a full democracy a bad form of government, because everything would turn to chaos due to the fact that all would have equal access to government without laws or reason. Likewise, monarchy would truly be the best only if there existed a perfect man who excelled above all else in virtue, intelligence, and honesty. Obviously, this could never be the case since no one like that humanly existed. In this case, Vitoria concludes that "the best polity nowadays is clearly the mixed, as Aquinas says. And this is more or less how it is, wherever there are kingdoms in Christendom" (In Pagden 1991, 199). Thus, in the end he agreed with Aquinas's "inconsistency."

Most scholars of Vitoria's time shared the idea that an organized system of laws and magistrates was necessary for the well-being and maintenance of a state, in order to avoid too many different interpretations. The rulers should be virtuous and apply these laws in accordance with the needs of a progressing civilization. In his *relectio*, "On Law," Vitoria posits the question, "Are judicial precepts of the Old Law perpetually binding?" (In Pagden 1991, 196). He answered the question by stating that you must "first define your times, and then you can make laws to fit them. Many things which are suitable for one people or country are not suitable for another" (In Pagden 1991, 196). This was an excellent point. However, these progressive ideas were not a permanent fixture in Vitoria's concepts. He fluctuated frequently between ideas and positions on his ideas, which at times could be disconcerting.

There are many more contradictions in this point of view. Who was designated as the voice of authority in debates about when Old Law should or should not be changed? What was considered a "virtuous law"? By whom?

Could there be, as we see today, a manipulation of the political process in the name of "morality"? Was the term "virtuous" used as a way of masking what the true, more superficial motives were? Can we claim a genuine concern to do what is right and only aspire to achieve what is truly good for all? Is this even efficient? Or do we see more the tendency to use this kind of terminology in discussing political matters in order to envelop the ugly truth in a deceptive cloak of false morality? As Brian Tierney states, "It is a mistake to see a concern for rights whenever we encounter policies that we may find morally congenial but that were really based on other grounds" (Tierney 2004, 2).

2.4 CIVIL POWER AND VITORIA'S CONCEPT OF STATE: *DE POTESTATE CIVILI* (ON CIVIL POWER 1528), *DE POTESTATE ECCLESIAE PRIOR* (ON CHURCH POWER I 1532), *DE POTESTATE ECCLESIAE POSTERIOR* (ON CHURCH POWER II 1533)

In order to understand fully Vitoria's jus gentium and his concept of just war, it is necessary to discuss his theory of state, because after all, the law of nations and the rules of war are essentially the rule of conduct among states. Vitoria's *relectio*, "On Civil Power" (1528), contains his essential theories on the state and the ethical problems linked to modern political statecraft. He discusses his concept of state and the nature of public and private power; he offers a defense of the monarchical system of Spain and a definition of a civil society and if and how the obligatory nature of civil laws should be regulated. His *relectio*, "On Church Power I" (1532), also presents crucial points on his concept of state formation and the separation of powers. His purposive concept of the state highlights the natural origin of political society and the authority governing it. He believed that the state, by founding its order and constitution of rights on justice, with the well-being and survival of its citizens as its objective, "provided its people with the foundations necessary for the flourishing of his individuality" (Valenzuela-Vermehren 2013, 93).

Two primary points shaped Vitoria's conception of state power: the fact that the state was founded in both natural and eternal laws and the idea that the state's civil laws could only be legitimate if they were the result of consent, human will, and legal enactment. A state was a "perfect community," meaning that it was complete, lacking in nothing, and this self-sufficiency allowed it to pursue its natural ends. Internally, it was independent of other states. It had its own laws, its own officials of the royal court, its own self-government, and the power resided in the individuals making up the state. Even though it was independent of foreign powers, a state was a member of the international community equal to others. Vitoria's definition of a perfect community can be found in his *relectio*, "On the Law of War," in which he states that "a perfect community or commonwealth is therefore one which is complete in itself; that is, one which is not part of another commonwealth, but has its own laws, its own independent policy, and its own magistrates" (In Pagden 1991, 301). He uses the kingdoms of Castile and Aragon as examples of perfect communities. This idea of a perfect community stems from Aquinas's theory on the two kinds of communities that existed. According to Aquinas, there was the imperfect community, such as the household which was part of another, greater community but was primarily concerned with its own private welfare, and the perfect community, such as a state which was self-sufficient and concerned with the well-being of all.

Vitoria began his discussion on this subject by asserting mankind's natural need for government. For him it was clear that "the primitive origin of human cities and commonwealths was not a human invention or contrivance to be numbered among the artifacts of craft, but a device implanted by Nature in man for his own safety and survival" (In Pagden 1991, 9). The source of states originated from nature. Given that states were "natural organisms," civil power had to have been invested first in the commonwealth and no individual could have held power prior to the states' formation. Vitoria and other political thinkers of this period used the traditional Aristotelian method of describing the origin of a community: human beings are naturally sociable and need society. To this was added the idea permeating Spanish thought during that time of God having designed man and woman for a community life, hence their gift of speech. Vitoria believed that people needed one another in order to be able to learn more and better themselves, and states and societies provided the environment in which they could practice their gifts of virtue and reason which only human beings possessed. The exercise of these unique gifts was what Vitoria called the final purpose or *telos*: "Every single atom exists for some use and purpose; and that everything must be as it is because of that purpose or *final cause*, which is the true reason and *necessary cause* of all things" (Emphasis in original) (In Pagden 1991, 6).

According to him, human societies were founded naturally, to lighten people's burdens by helping each other and creating strength in numbers. Here is where Vitoria's idea of the mutual obligation of humans toward one another comes to light. He considered this perfectly normal and it did not need to be written down as a law. He expressed the innate need of mankind to have a commonwealth order, since this derives from divine and natural law. In other words, community was not an artificial creation by man, but rather a natural, sociohistorical phenomenon, and the obligation of humans toward one another was also natural and instinctive.

As mentioned previously, Vitoria distinguishes between authority and power. Power rests in a community of individuals and becomes authority when it is transferred to a ruler. This does not mean that the community *creates* the power; the power as an entity has come from God and the community simply picks the instrument by which this power will be exercised. Though the commonwealth has power by divine law over the individual members of the commonwealth, as has been proved, it is impossible for this power to be administered by the commonwealth itself, that is to say, by the multitude. Therefore, it is necessary that the government and administration of affairs be entrusted to certain individuals who assume the responsibilities of the commonwealth and look after the common good. The power in the community, once it has been transferred to the ruler, is irrevocable and the commonwealth does not keep any of it.

Vitoria does assert that once the power has been transferred from the community to the king, although the king is now the head of the commonwealth and the executor of human law, the legislative power itself still rests in the commonwealth. In other words, even though the king is the executor of human law, he is still subject to the same laws that he makes. Although he is, according to Vitoria, "over the whole commonwealth, he is nevertheless part of the commonwealth" (In Pagden 1991, 181). Vitoria did acknowledge, however, that even though the king had to follow his own laws just as the commonwealth did, if he did break one, his sin was not equal to that of the commonwealth if the law was broken "because he compensates for it by holding other and greater burdens in the interest of the commonwealth" (In Pagden 1991, 182). This exception is very contradictory. If the king shares the same obligation to follow the law as his subjects, neither should he be exempt from punishment nor should his sin be lessened when he does not follow it. This idea of being above the law has, unfortunately, been the reality of all political leaders throughout time and continues to be the case in the present.

Vitoria does, albeit reluctantly, concede that the king's power is revocable when used tyrannically or negatively toward the commonwealth: "If a king proves to be a tyrant in government the commonwealth can depose him, because even if the commonwealth has given away its authority, it keeps its natural right to defend itself; if there is no other way, it may reject its king" (In Pagden 1991, 200). This is an adaptation of a Roman doctrine that law could be permissive and did not only consist of restraints of power and authority but also a certain degree of flexibility where people, more specifically agents of the law, were free to act as they saw fit in a particular situation. French theologian Jean Gerson, who promoted church reform in the 1400s, advocated for this natural right of self-defense against a tyrannical pope as well. Overall, however, the safety and stability of the commonwealth was such a high priority for Vitoria that even under a tyrant, whose laws were usually not binding since he had no legitimate power, the state should follow the laws if the commonwealth at that time has no way to make new laws or enforce them. Their only means of survival as a state was to follow a set of laws, wherever those may come from. This is where Vitoria contradicts himself from the previous statement he made that the commonwealth, even though it loses the power once it has been transferred, still possesses the right to self-defense and in the case of a king becoming a tyrant has the right to depose him. He goes as far as stating that "utility and respect are better served by obedience to a tyrant's laws than by disobedience to all law" (In Pagden 1991, 42). He believed that an anarchical commonwealth run by no laws would meet a far worse fate (its doom and dismantlement) than if they at least have some organizational structure and laws, even those coming from a tyrant. Obviously, for Vitoria, the safety, well-being, and duration of a commonwealth were the most important elements in the preservation of a state and its people. The security of the commonwealth was crucial for the state's survival and progress and the primary objective of civil power was to provide this natural need for an organized distribution of power. Thus, his idea of the inalienable human power and freedom to make law is counteracted by the obligation of mankind to obey all laws.

A primary requisite for Vitoria's perfect state was its self-government and independence from other governments. This idea of sovereign independence and the ability to serve and protect the people of the community as primary traits of the foundation of the state was quickly accepted in political and legal thought around the world. Essentially, he described a state as a group of human beings residing in more or less marked territory with internal sovereignty and independence of foreign control, and a political organization through which the collective will of the population could be expressed and enforced. The following are the fundamental characteristics of Vitoria's concept of a legitimate state: a collection of human beings with a governing power elected by that community and assigned to look after their well-being and safety; all governing power of the state came from God; the majority ruled; and laws and constitutions of rulers were binding to all, even those who made them. Vitoria argued that the American Indians matched these criteria and had legitimate states, and therefore were a part of the international community and subject to the law of nations. This modern concept demonstrates that Vitoria's concept of international community was not necessarily representative of a common religion, but rather of a common humanity.

2.5 VITORIA "ON CHURCH POWER" (I-1532, II-1533)

During the twelfth century, the immensely powerful codification of church law in Gratian's *Decretum* was followed by the creation of a new structure of universal jurisprudence for the church. Vitoria discusses this new hierarchical structure in his *relectio*, "On Church Power," which is also essential to the understanding of his idea of the power of state, its formation, and the separation of the powers of church and state. He stated that spiritual power was held only by the church, and this power, although thought of as higher on the hierarchical scale than the power of the state, was still expected to work in accordance with natural and civil laws and aim toward the ultimate objective: the common good for all and individual happiness. Spiritual power was considered more valuable than civil power in the sense that its ultimate purpose was guiding the individual to eternal life. Spiritual power dealt with supernatural and eternal matters and its ultimate objective was individual happiness, whereas the objective of civil power was social happiness.

Spiritual power was in charge of regulating things that were incomprehensible to the "common man," things that could not be known without religious revelation, such as the forgiveness of sins and the consecration of the Holy Eucharist, whereas civil power primarily concerned itself with the well-being of the state and community. According to Vitoria, "The purpose of spiritual power far excels that of temporal power, in the measure that perfect bliss and ultimate felicity excel all human or earthly happiness" (In Pagden 1991, 82). He believed that spiritual power not only did not originate from civil law but also existed independently from natural law, which heretofore may have been seen as an umbrella under which all other laws fit. He explains that since natural law can only include the powers of nature and does not exceed its limits, it is impossible for it to extend as far as the spiritual realm. The same applies to civil law.

Once again, Vitoria adds some confusing exceptions, making a distinction between spiritual power, which has always existed in the church, and ecclesiastical power, which is necessary to carry out the spiritual power and parts of which could have come from natural and/or human law: "Ecclesiastical power might, in some of its aspects, have arisen from natural or positive law, that is in some effects and actions of its power" (In Pagden 1991, 71). The distinction between spiritual power and ecclesiastical power is not made very clear in Vitoria's writings. They seem to coexist and are best explained in "On the Power of the Church I":

> Spiritual power has existed from the beginning. And this is confirmed by the fact that the Church, as a spiritual community ordained towards a supernatural end, has always existed; but no commonwealth can be self-sufficient (*perfecta*) without magistracies and authorities, therefore ecclesiastical power has always existed. (In Pagden 1991, 75)

By this definition, ecclesiastical power is the organization and governing of spiritual power and both are always working together.

Vitoria further states that the pope was, without a doubt, supreme ruler of all ecclesiastical power, but was not "lord of the whole world" due to the fact that his powers were not omnipresent but were concentrated solely in the spiritual realm. The main reason for this was that it would be impossible for one man to carry such a heavy weight of authority on his shoulders. It would be too much responsibility and require unlimited knowledge, a human impossibility: "No single man would ever be capable of fulfilling all the administrative duties of both the ecclesiastical and civil commonwealths, or of learning the separate disciplines involved in each" (In Pagden 1991, 52).

Not surprisingly, Vitoria illustrates an exception to this situation. A time when civil power would be subject to the pope's spiritual power and when the pope would have the authority to make laws outside of the particular realm of natural and divine laws was when some civil policy was proving to be detrimental to the spiritual ministry. However, Vitoria emphasized that this was only the case if the situation in question involved the saving of souls: "So long as a thing is not incompatible with the salvation of souls and religion, the pope's office is not involved" (In Pagden 1991, 95). However, this "exception" to the rule is one that is not so clearly delineated and that could easily be manipulated to one's own advantage. Detrimental to the spiritual ministry? That was a pretty hefty veto card! Did Vitoria not realize this? Or did he? The church and pope would then have the power to claim whatever they chose as "incompatible with the salvation of souls" even though this may not really be the case. Therefore, in a sense, the church actually did possess temporal power and authority over the whole world, but under the disguise of being done "only to achieve spiritual ends." However, in his *relectio*, "On Civil Power," Vitoria switches things up again by taking a moment to reflect on Aquinas's argument and disagreeing with it in this respect: "I cannot believe that when St Thomas wrote *ST* III he was a partisan of the fantastic notion that emperors are vicars of Christ in temporal matters. . . . I think this is untrue of purely temporal power" (In Pagden 1991, 28).

He ended his discussion on the distinction between civil and church powers by reiterating that neither the emperors nor the pope were rulers of the world. Their authority was partial, with popes belonging to the spiritual and emperors to the civil realm. The existence of distinctive realms of power with their own rulers was vital to the well-being and survival of the state. However, we find yet another inconsistency in Vitoria's thought when he states later in this *relectio*, "I assert that the pope has the widest power: that is, whenever and to whatever degree it may be necessary for spiritual ends, he has not only the powers which the secular princes have, but also the power to make new princes, to unmake others, to divide empires, and other such things" (In

Pagden 1991, 93). In other words, all the powers that Vitoria had previously limited or denied to the pope are given right back to them under this "deceptive cloak of false morality," the presupposition of protecting the church and the word of God. Which means that the powers of the pope are never really *taken away* but just masked by a different terminology, for almost anything could be manipulated to have a "spiritual objective." If it came down to it and there were, for example, a duel between temporal and spiritual power, the latter would be the victor with no hesitation. For in the end, regardless of Vitoria's confusing descriptions and definitions, he concludes that "temporal matters exist for spiritual ones and depend on them" (In Pagden 1991, 91).

Vitoria believed that life needed to be regulated by these powers, civil and spiritual, separately and jointly, each working on their own level, but working in harmony with and complementing one another. The individuality of these powers was very important for Vitoria who concluded, with many supporting quotes from the Bible, that the differences between church and state power not only existed but were inevitable and even beneficial for the common good. Vitoria's use of God as an authoritative source for this argument leaves it pretty irrefutable. He claims that the distinction between these two powers was designed explicitly by God in accordance with the order of the world. He skillfully uses examples from both the New and Old Testaments to support his claim and virtually bombards the reader with biblical passages to the point that one becomes convinced of the validity of this argument.

Within the church, there was a further division of power: sacramental, concerning the true body of Christ and the Eucharist, and jurisdictional power, which concerned the mythical body of Christ and guiding Christian people toward their "supernatural happiness." According to Vitoria, the internal structure of the church was similar to that of society and he described it as "nothing other than a sort of commonwealth of all Christians" (In Pagden 1991, 111). Both possessed an internal hierarchy and had certain ranks of power. The one big difference, however, lay in the power invested and distributed in both realms. Vitoria strongly emphasizes the distinction between the church's distribution of power and that of the people. This is another one of his arguments that is slightly confusing and can leave the reader with less of an idea of what he was discussing than before they started to read his argument. He stated that the spiritual power of the church "neither was in the beginning, nor is in itself or indeed in any other way whatsoever, vested immediately in the whole universal Church, in the way in which civil power is vested in the commonwealth" (In Pagden 1991, 114). This introduction is not the confusing part, it is very straightforward and to the point, but it is the mass of supporting arguments that follow that is mind-boggling. Instead of clarifying anything, he leaves things floating in a sea of ambiguity with nothing to grasp onto for a better understanding. After several readings, I was able to make my way through this labyrinth and retrieve his relatively simple conclusion.

Vitoria's idea of the difference between church and state power is essentially that the power of the church comes directly from God, whereas the authority of the king is derived from the people, who in turn received it from God. During the twelfth century, Thomas Beckett had famously defended the rights of the church against powerful kings which in turn is asserted in the Magna Carta: "The English Church shall be free, and shall have all its rights entire" (Holt 1992, 449). Vitoria explains that "this power belongs to the whole Church either by natural law, or by human, or by divine law; but in fact it does not belong to the Church by any of these laws" (In Pagden 1991, 115). This leaves things in a very indefinite state. He follows by clarifying, "Ecclesiastical power goes beyond both human and natural law, both as regards to the purpose for which it is ordained, which is supernatural, and as regards to its effect, which is all human capability, consisting as it does in the remission of sins, the conferral of grace, and the consecration of the Eucharist" (In Pagden 1991, 115). Does this exclude divine law? Would it not seem normal that the power of the church would come from divine law? Vitoria argued that this was definitely not the case: "As for divine law, it is clear that this power cannot belong to the Church by divine law because all this power has its sole author, our Lord and Savior Jesus Christ" (In Pagden 1991, 115).

He traced the lineage from the first twelve disciples and said that the first apostles did get their sacramental and jurisdictional powers not from the church but from Christ himself and this was then in turn passed on to their successors. In fact, according to Vitoria, no one but the apostles received their ecclesiastical power directly from Christ. Ecclesiastical power did not come from the church and was not vested in the entire church, but rather "is given in first instance to certain persons, and through them belongs to the Church" (In Pagden 1991, 124). Out of the twelve apostles, Peter was the "supreme prince of the Church"; he was, as Vitoria describes, the "first and prince of all the apostles in authority and power, with supreme power over the whole Church" (In Pagden 1991, 137). This is similar to Cajetan's argument that Peter had the sole jurisdictional authority out of the apostles, in addition to their equal sacramental power which they all held individually. Somewhat confusingly, Vitoria later argued that after the death of the apostles, their power was vested in the church and that the supreme pontiff of the church was not to be elected by a select few men, but by the whole church, which sounds very similar to the process of the distribution of power from the commonwealth to its ruler, a similarity that Vitoria refutes emphatically but which exists nonetheless. The pope is the one who has the power of Peter passed down to him as a subrogate. Since Peter had died without mentioning a specific successor, the church had inherited the power to institute someone in Peter's place. However, since this successor would have universal power as well, he must be chosen by the whole church, not just by a particular individual or group of men.

Vitoria also made sure to exclude women from having any role of power in the church. In his opinion, "all ecclesiastical orders and powers are ordained for the governance and direction of the populace to spiritual ends; and these things cannot be suited to a woman" (In Pagden 1991, 130). Now, although he never directly states why this may not be so or what women may have done to prove themselves unworthy of holding power in the church, he does extract various quotes from the Bible as his proof, for example, from letters of St. Paul to the Corinthians, "Let your women keep silence in the churches, for it is not permitted unto them to speak, but they are commanded to be under obedience; and if they will learn anything, let them ask their husbands at home, for it is a shame for women to speak in the church," and from Timothy, "Let the woman learn in silence with all subjection; but I suffer not a woman to teach, nor to usurp authority over the man, but to be in silence," as well as from others (In Pagden 1991, 130). This sounds remarkably similar to his argument on the negative and subservient condition of the American Indians. As can be seen, Vitoria himself offered nothing as to why this has to be the case or any circumstantial evidence supporting this theory. At the end of this long passage quoting numerous biblical authoritative figures on the idea, he concluded with what he claimed was the most convincing argument of all, the fact that it had never been done before:

> What convinces me the most is the fact that in all the long process of the years, and with all the abundance of good, wise women, the Church has never tried to raise any woman to ecclesiastical power or office. For me it is always a powerful argument in this and in other cases, when a thing has never been done despite abundant opportunity and occasion for doing it, to assume that it has not been done because it was not lawful or possible. (In Pagden 1991, 130)

This sounds very conservative and traditional, contrasting sharply with his relatively liberal previous argument that things that have always been so in the Old Law had no reason to keep being so because the laws and customs change with the times of a progressing civilization. Vitoria even offends the female gender and indirectly invokes the original sin of Eve in making his point about the exclusion of women: "It would be very dangerous to entrust the spiritual salvation of souls to a person who was unable to discriminate between what is good and what is harmful to the salvation of souls" (In Pagden 1991, 131).

The impending threat of the Protestant Reformation and the teachings of Martin Luther were also tackled by Vitoria in his discussions on church power. He demeaned everything that had anything to do with Luther's ideas and did so with a sharp bite (describing Luther as the "most impudent" of the modernists). For example, when addressing the question of whether ecclesiastical power was vested in all Christians or only given to a select few he argued that

> the modernists have taken it upon themselves in their arrogance to contradict the Church's universally accepted opinion, contentiously asserting that all Christians are rightfully priests, and that there exist no ecclesiastical orders in the Church. However, they do not strive officiously to prove their point with arguments or texts. As is their way, they simply pluck some passage or other from Scripture, twist it to their purpose, and then, with the bit of heresy firmly between their teeth, go forth and spread dissent and fraction. (In Pagden 1991, 126)

The last line is very illustrative of Vitoria's skill as a writer and the manner in which he colorfully and somewhat passionately expressed his ideas. One of Vitoria's many problems with Luther's idea was that for Luther there existed no hierarchy of power in the church. In his *relectio*, "On the Power of the Church II," Vitoria addresses this point directly and questions that if that were the case, then how could there be any stability? Or, as he put it, "If Luther thinks we are all eyes, then where are the feet?" (In Pagden 1991, 128). The organization of church power was crucial for Vitoria, who believed that without it, there would just be a confused mob of men acting out their own whims and pleasures. Vitoria and Luther's biggest difference was in the way they viewed the power of the church. For Luther, true faith was a question of spiritual subjectivity; man's body was his own private church. Vitoria, on the other hand, saw religion as more of an institutional concept, with a hierarchy and the pope at the head of the church.

Vitoria's view on law (natural, divine, human, etc.), his idea of a state, and his position on the power of the church serve to come to a better understanding of the arguments that he presents in *De Jure Belli* and *De indis* and the thought process involved in reaching his conclusions. *De indis*, focused primarily on the question and rights of the American Indians, illustrates Vitoria's fundamental notions of law, church, and state, which come together to formulate his concept of human rights.

Chapter 3

Vitoria

On the American Indians (De Indis Prior)

Vitoria's *relectio*, "De Indis reenter invenitur relectio prior" (On the American Indians), which he delivered in 1539, expresses his ideas on human rights and people's obligation toward one another, the concept of the barbarian, and colonial relationship. The latter refers specifically to the lawfulness by which the American Indians were subjected to Spanish rule, the question of powers the Spanish had over the American Indians in temporal and civil matters, and the authority of the church and the monarchy in religious matters. Vitoria also offers an analysis of Spanish hegemony and poses the highly debated question of the right and legitimacy of subjecting the American Indians subject to Spanish rule. This question gave way to another important one: Did the American Indians possess true dominion over their own property and affairs before the arrival of the Spaniards? According to Gratian, by natural law all property was common and any human law contrary to natural law was illegal and void. In that case, how could the fact that property was privatized in the real world be justified?

De Indis was, at the time, a thorough and groundbreaking discussion of the rights of the American Indians in the New World. Before then, the way in which the Spanish Crown had justified its claim to the New World had been through the Bulls of Donation made by Pope Alexander VI, granting the Spanish Crown possession of all non-Christian inhabited lands. Vitoria refuted this claim on the grounds that the pope did not have such temporal authority and legitimized the Spanish presence in the New World by presenting a theory that assigned certain religious responsibilities to temporal authorities.

De Indis is divided into three sections. The first section addresses the question of whether the children of unbelievers may be baptized against the wishes of their parents, and Vitoria centers his reply on the Gospel text of

Matthew 28:19: "Teach all nations, baptizing them in the name of the Father and of the Son and of the Holy Spirit." In the second section, Vitoria discusses illegitimate reasons for Spanish sovereignty that he refers to as titles, such as the emperor being Lord of the whole world or the pope holding full jurisdiction in temporal matters. This section is the one where Vitoria spends the majority of his time on the question of the American Indians' rights and their dominion, especially on whether or not the American Indians possessed true dominion over their own property before the arrival of the Spaniards.[1] He argues that they did, because dominion is attached to every human being as a gift from God since the day of creation. Therefore, any power or dominion that existed must be attributed ultimately to God. Vitoria does point out, however, that whereas dominion belongs to all human beings through divine law, the distribution of it belongs to human law in relation to private property, which was not that egalitarian.

In the third section, Vitoria examines reasons that might be legitimate for the Spanish conquest, such as natural society and fellowship. For him, visitors and foreigners should be treated well as long as they are respectful themselves. For him this title was based on the natural order of the world; the freedom of circulation of ideas, goods, and people ultimately served the common good by helping to formulate and increase sentiments of "universal brotherhood." In order to analyze these three concepts thoroughly, Vitoria included a lengthy discussion, very insightful for his time, on the nature and societies of the natives, addressing their rituals, traditions, and customs.[2] He does this to prove that the American Indians could not be termed "madmen" or "irrational." They did possess reason and therefore also had rights and true dominion, both public and private. This portion of Vitoria's discussion will be further analyzed later in this chapter.

In the end, Vitoria stripped each supposed title for Spanish dominion in the New World so bare that he left the Crown with little to work with and no firm stand on which to justify the conquest of Indian Territory in the New World. He left the Crown with a slight claim to jurisdiction in the Americas but took away all legitimate property rights. However, seemingly aware of this, he did conclude his lecture stating that since the Spanish were already there, financially it would do more harm than good to the Spanish Empire to leave, and this of course was no option. There are striking parallels here with present-day situations such as presidents Kennedy and Johnson in Vietnam, President Bush in Iraq, and President Obama in Afghanistan. As Vitoria expresses, "If all these titles were inapplicable, that is to say if the barbarians gave no just cause for war and did not wish to have the Spaniards as princes and so on, *the whole Indian expedition and trade would cease*, to the great loss of the Spaniards. And this in turn would mean a huge loss to the royal exchequer, which would be intolerable" (Emphasis in original) (In Pagden 1991, 291).

3.1 ILLEGITIMATE TITLES

In this part of Vitoria's *relectio*, he lists seven titles that were not legitimate for the Spanish conquest. The first two were that neither the emperor nor the pope were masters of the world: "Dominion can exist only by natural law, divine law, or human law. But the emperor is not master of the world by any of these" (In Pagden 1991, 253). Since by natural law all men were free and equal, no one could be emperor over all others directly under natural law. In regard to divine law, Vitoria argues that emperors being "masters of the world" before the advent of Christ was not written anywhere: "If the emperor was master by divine law, how did the empire come to be divided into its western and eastern components?" (In Pagden 1991, 256). Here he makes an interesting reference to Noah as the initial colonizer, claiming that after the Flood he had sent out expeditions to colonize the different regions of the earth, dividing the world into various kingdoms and countries, thereby making it impossible that anyone before Christ could have obtained an empire by divine law or had become emperor of the world. Vitoria also says that this division of the world into different kingdoms and countries could have been done by the mutual consent of the nations as well, as different groups colonized different areas.

In the case of human law, Vitoria argues that the emperor could definitely not have universal jurisdiction under this law because there would need to be an enactment for this to be the case and this did not exist. He claims that even if the emperor were ruler of the world, the American Indians would still possess their own dominion and the emperor would not be entitled to occupy the lands of the natives or remove their rulers and replace them with new ones, or even impose taxes on them.

Second, Vitoria argues that the pope is not the civil or temporal master of the world either. His first proof of this comes from the fact that in his decree *Per uenerabilem*, Innocent III had stated that he had no powers in temporal matters over the king of France. Vitoria argues that since the pope had no temporal power over the "barbarians" either, he could not declare war on them because they refused to recognize any dominion of his. Here is where Vitoria is also very clear about the fact that even if the American Indians did not and would not recognize Christ as their lord, this was not enough reason to go to war against them and take away their land and possessions. He uses the example of the Saracens who were able to live among the Christians in relative peace without being stripped of their belongings and goods: "It would be harsh to deny to them, who have never done us any wrong, the rights we concede to Saracens and Jews, who have been continual enemies of the Christian religion" (In Pagden 1991, 251). To solidify this argument even more, Vitoria uses authoritative figures such as Silvestro Mazzolini da

Priero, Thomas Aquinas, and Cajetan. According to Vitoria, "there is no doctor, even among our adversaries, who concedes the argument that they may be despoiled solely on the grounds of unbelief" (In Pagden 1991, 263).

Third, according to Vitoria, the possessions of these lands by right of discovery were completely unjustified, because the American Indians were there first. This argument is quite short and concise: "The law of nations, on the other hand, expressly states that goods which belong to no owner pass to the occupier. Since the goods in question have had an owner, they do not fall under this title" (In Pagden 1991, 265).

In his discussion on the illegitimate reasons for the Spanish conquest, Vitoria clarifies that there only existed four reasons why the American Indians would not have been "true masters" of their own property and possessions before the arrival of the Spaniards: if they were sinners (*peccatores*), unbelievers (*infideles*), madmen (*amentes*), or insensates (*insensate*). He goes into length to show that the American Indians' status did not fit any of them. Vitoria did not try to argue that the American Indians were not sinners or unbelievers but rather focused on the fact that even as sinners, they could not be deprived of their dominion and land because, as he claims, "mortal sin is no impediment to the civil right of ownership, nor to true dominion. This was one of the propositions determined by the Council of Constance" (In Pagden 1991, 241). Vitoria also claims that the rights of pagan princes with respect to the administration of their territories and powers could not be argued.

Vitoria's fourth illegitimate reason for the Spanish conquest was that the American Indians had refused to accept the faith of Christ. This part of Vitoria's discussion becomes very repetitive, as he speaks quite at length about this illegitimate title, shrouding the same basic idea and argument in different terminology. Vitoria argues that the American Indians had never before received any news of Christ or of the Christian faith, so they did not know who the Spanish were or what they had come to preach. For this part of his discussion, Vitoria raises the opposing arguments of figures such as William of Auxerre, William of Auvergne, Jean Gerson, and Hugh of St. Victor, all of whom basically stated that it is impossible for anyone to live in complete ignorance of God for He would reveal himself to them and enlighten them. Vitoria argues that this cannot be the case, for those who live in complete ignorance of something cannot be committing a sin for not believing in it. He points out that "it is extraordinary to claim that an unbeliever, or indeed anyone in a state of mortal sin, cannot be invincibly ignorant about any matter whatsoever in divine law" (In Pagden 1991, 268). For him, the only way this ignorance could be considered a sin would be if it were accompanied by some form of negligence, such as a refusal to listen or a refusal to believe once one has heard the word of God. He uses the argument and authority of St. Paul to support this theory: "How shall they believe in him of whom they have not yet heard? And how shall they hear without a preacher?" (In Pagden 1991, 267).

Vitoria makes an interesting point in this fourth illegitimate title: "When there are no miraculous signs or other reasons for belief, there will be no sin" (In Pagden 1991, 270). The fact that the American Indians did not believe in God after simply being told about Him was not a sin. Why should they believe something that had not been proven but simply stated? They are not obliged to believe without proof but are obliged to listen when this proof is offered to them. However, no persuasive proof had been offered to the American Indians yet. It was actually more the other way around. He blames this not on the friars, preachers, and other officials of the church, but on others with more selfish motives:

> On the contrary, I hear only of provocations, savage crimes, and multitudes of unholy acts. From this, it does not appear that the Christian religion has been preached to them in a sufficiently pious way to oblige their acquiescence; even though it is clear that a number of friars and other churchmen have striven industriously in this cause, by the example of their lives and the diligence of their preaching, and this would have been enough, had they not been thwarted by others with different aims. (In Pagden 1991, 271)

In the case of the American Indians as unbelievers, Vitoria follows closely the argument of Aquinas that unbelief did not cancel out either natural or human law. This point of Vitoria is the strongest of the four, and he offers again the example of the Jews and Saracens to strengthen his argument: "It is clear that it is not lawful to take away the possessions of Saracens, Jews, or other unbelievers on the ground of their unbelief *per se*; to do so is theft or robbery, no less than it would be in the case of Christians" (In Pagden 1991, 244).

Even though Vitoria agrees that neither madmen nor irrational people could have natural rights or possess property, this was clearly not the case with respect to the American Indians and could not be used as a reason for conquering them and their land. The fact that the American Indians were different did not mean that they were irrational. Rather, the American Indians had well-organized cities and societies, laws, commerce, and religion, among other things. By emphasizing their humanity, Vitoria introduces a significant change to the traditional view of the indigenous as creatures of nature. Every human being is rational by nature and is entitled to be treated as such, even if he is a sinner. He can therefore not be robbed from either his natural rights or property.

Vitoria concludes his lengthy discussion on the fourth illegitimate reason for the Spanish conquest by stating that even if the Christian faith had been preached to the American Indians in the best possible way and was still rejected by them, this was still not a good enough reason to declare war on them. Citing St. Thomas again he argues that unbelievers who have never taken up the faith cannot be compelled by force to believe. Vitoria, using again the examples of the Saracens and Jews, claims that "Christians" who are compelled to believe by force are the worst kind: "Belief is a matter of will but fear considerably diminishes the freedom of will. To come to the mysteries and sacraments of Christ merely out of servile fear would be sacrilege" (In Pagden 1991, 272). Vitoria did not only follow St. Thomas's argument that faith could and should never be imposed by force and that neither sin nor disbelief could take away a man's natural rights but also used writings of authoritative figures such as St. Gregory the Great and the conclusions reached at the Council of Trent to solidify his argument even more.

The fifth illegitimate title rested on the supposed sins of the barbarians. Vitoria argues that, contrary to popular belief, the American Indians could not be attacked due to their sins against natural law, such as incest or sodomy. Christian princes did not have such authority because the Spanish were not rulers over the entire world, however much they would have liked to be. As Vitoria states, paraphrasing St. Thomas, "Prelates have received power only over those who have subjected themselves to the faith" (In Pagden 1991, 274).

Vitoria's sixth illegitimate reason for the Spanish conquest is that it was not the choice of the American Indians. This argument is not as complex as his previous one and he basically states that this could definitely not be the case, because the American Indians could not agree to accept that which they did not understand:

> This title, too, is inapplicable. This is clear, first of all, because the choice ought not to have been made in fear and ignorance, factors which vitiate any freedom of election, but which played a leading part in this particular choice and acceptance. The barbarians do not realize what they are doing; perhaps, indeed, they do not even understand what it is the Spaniards are asking of them. Besides which, the request is made by armed men, who surround a fearful and defenseless crowd. (In Pagden 1991, 276)

This very concise argument is truly refreshing, after having read several of his more characteristic long-winded discussions.

Vitoria's last illegitimate title is that of the Americas being a special gift from God. Here Vitoria simply states that this was definitely not the case, because God would not have given rights to the American Indians if He planned on having them taken away later, and He would never deprive any man of his natural rights.

As mentioned in the previous chapter, Vitoria did not agree entirely with Aristotle's theory of natural slaves, but rather than contradicting it, he reformulated it in order to harmonize it with his own ideologies. By relating to Aristotle's premises instead of his conclusions, Vitoria was able to mold Aristotle's point of view so that it would fit his own.[3]

In the opinion of many intellectuals of the period, such as Juan Ginés de Sepúlveda, the American Indians fit the Aristotelian natural slave/barbarian category perfectly and since they were inferior beings, they could not exercise natural or property rights. Vitoria rejected this claim arguing that although the Indian culture may not be as civilized as the Spanish, this was not due to their lack of rationality but to their primitive upbringing, which made them seem not fully rational creatures. The Spaniards believed that their cultural and intellectual superiority made them superior to the American Indians. However, according to Vitoria, the American Indians did have full possession over their rights. This argument is contradictory to his previous statements that the "barbarians" possessed reason and "judgment like other men," proven by the order and organization of their own affairs. Now, their status was made similar to that of a child, in which case Vitoria states that the Crown *might* be able to take over the lands of the American Indians and make the American Indians themselves their subjects until they reached an "age of reason," in that sense becoming their tutors and helping them reach a more civilized level of life. This is one of his legitimate titles to Spanish dominion discussed later. He was somewhat hesitant about this claim but did justify it as a charitable act that should be done by neighbors. This theory of the American Indians' "infantism" was not a unique concept at the time. Christopher Columbus and Bartolomé de Las Casas also believed that the American Indians should be treated as "innocents," naive to the world and in need of instruction. The question is, Who decided when that "age of reason" came? What were to be the distinguishing factors that would let one know when the American Indians had matured enough to be able to exercise their dominion rights? And under which authority?

In spite of these occasional incongruences, it is impressive that Vitoria defended the property rights of the natives against the imposition of an imperial power at a time when questioning the Crown's use of power was atypical. Even though Vitoria may have had other reasons in mind that did not necessarily include the well-being of the American Indians, this does not diminish the uniqueness of his position on the subject of imperial power. He was indeed open-minded for his time, regardless of his tendency to overidealize many of his concepts and to contradict himself. He championed the rights of all human beings to be equal members of the international community. Nevertheless, it is important to keep in mind also other perspectives on Vitoria's "progressive" concept of universal, natural, human rights. According to Brian Tierney,

"There is no consensus in modern writing about Vitoria's teaching on natural rights. . . . Some maintained that Vitoria and his followers, as good Thomists, did not teach a doctrine of subjective rights, but adhered faithfully to the objective sense of *ius* defined by Aquinas" (Tierney 1997, 257). However, the predominant view on this matter is the one that scholar Richard Tuck proposes: that Vitoria was actually able to undermine the institution of slavery by drastically limiting the legitimate conditions under which men could become slaves. Vitoria recognized that civil law may permit the ownership of some by others, but under natural law, there were no legitimate grounds for slavery.

Overall, for Vitoria the fact that the American Indians were non-Christians did not contradict natural law, on which ownership and dominion were founded, and therefore did not prevent anyone from being the rightful owner of his possessions and land. He argued that every human being had a right to dominion through divine law and this was not subject to human interference of any kind. Not even mortal sin hindered true dominion. Any claim that the Spaniards wanted to make on the American Indians and their territory would have to be done in spite of natural law. Even if it were human law that determined their status, human rights could not be abused due to a failure to follow divine law. The American Indians were free people by nature and possessed legitimate property that the Spaniards had no right to take. In John Killoran's "Aquinas and Vitoria: Two Perspectives on Slavery," he argues that "these claims preclude the possibility of natural slavery, for a being who has command over himself (and persons, whether Indian or Europeans, pagans or Christians, do have command over themselves) cannot be enslaved as he is made in the image of God" (Killoran 1987, 94).

3.2 LEGITIMATE TITLES

Vitoria offered seven legitimate reasons for Spanish domination and in the end almost reluctantly adds an eighth. Many of these also have become ethical reasons for a just war. His first just title had to do with natural partnership and communication. This was his strongest argument out of the eight. The reason that Vitoria most supported for the Spaniards to go to the New World was the right of free travel and natural partnership. This argument can be seen as his primary justification of the expansion of the Spanish Empire into the New World and was strongly influenced by the Dominicans' ideal of an international world order where all humans were equal by natural law. Interestingly, Antony Anghie argued that Vitoria's universal natural law was really nothing more than "the particular cultural practices of the Spanish, unilaterally taken to a universal level" (Anghie 1999, 332).

Vitoria states that the Spaniards have the right to travel and live in those countries, as long as they do not harm the native inhabitants. He also uses a quote from the Scriptures, "Every living creature loveth his like," and twists it to suit his argument by explaining that "amity between men is a part of natural law, and it is against nature to shun the company of harmless men" (In Pagden 1991, 279). When he refers to harmless men, of whom exactly is he speaking? The Spaniards? Surely he cannot be describing their presence in the New World as harmless, especially after being aware of the horrific events that had taken place in Peru and in other places at the hands of the conquistadores. He employs the "love thy neighbor" argument, to which he quite comfortably refers throughout his lecture, using the authority of Matthew's Gospel to defend his idea that the indigenous are obliged to love their neighbors as themselves. Does this include neighbors that pillage, ransack, rape, murder, take, and destroy the other neighbors' things? Did Vitoria not take this into account or did he simply idealize and gloss over the situation as he often tended to do? For this title, Vitoria also argues that the Spaniards have the right to trade with the American Indians so long as the Spaniards commit no crimes or do no harm to the American Indians and to their land. This is yet another idealistic Vitorian argument. Obviously, that was neither taking place nor did it look like it would be any time soon, and it lacked any kind of legitimacy. As Toy-Fung Tung interestingly describes, "Vitoria's infamous claims of free travel, unfettered preaching, and the right to scoop up Amerindian gems reveal the potentially lawless core of his commonwealth order" (Tung 2014, 4).

The second legitimate title that Vitoria adduced for the Spanish presence in the Americas was for the spreading of the Christian religion: "Christians have the right to preach and announce the Gospel in the lands of the barbarians" (In Pagden 1991, 284). I found this second title to be very interesting in the way it gave back to the pope some, if not most, of the powers that Vitoria had taken away from him in his *relectio* "On Church Power." Vitoria does not necessarily give back those powers directly but rather masks them under a different terminology, a characteristic talent of his, introducing so many exceptions to the general rule that it waters it down completely. In this case, the exception is that spiritual power could always overtake other laws for its own survival and progress. Not only that, but he also says that the pope may make new princes "for the furtherance of religion, especially in places where there had never before been any Christian prince" (In Pagden 1991, 85). In this part of his discussion, he does reiterate the claim that if the American Indians let the Spaniards come into their lands and preach the Gospel and trade without hindering them, even if they did not accept the Christian religion, this was still no reason to go to war against them. However, if they did try to stop the Spaniards from enjoying their right of "natural partnership and communication," then this gave the Spaniards the justification to go up in arms against them. This was yet another example of wording that could easily be manipulated to fit more selfish needs.

The third legitimate title was for the protection of converts. This argument is very much to the point and again refers to the idea of a "universal brotherhood" and "love thy neighbor." If the American Indians had converted to Christ and their rulers tried to call them back to their paganistic ways, then the Spaniards had the authority to wage war on the rulers in order to convince them to stop and to "protect" the new converts: "The barbarians are all our neighbors, and therefore anyone, and especially princes, may defend them from such tyranny and oppression" (In Pagden 1991, 288).

The fourth legitimate reason consisted of a papal constitution of a Christian prince, by which the pope was given the power on "reasonable grounds" to remove the American Indians' "infidel" masters and give them a Christian prince whether the American Indians had asked him to do so or not. Once again, Vitoria contradicts his previous argument that the pope did not have this power. It is becoming evident that Vitoria at first states a series of "illegitimate titles" and reasons that the Spaniards could not use to conquer the American Indians and take over their land, but then he adds such a great number of amendments to these restrictions, that in the end they cease to be limiting. Vitoria seemed to be aware of this "problem" and explained that these exceptions to nonintervention were only to be done in cases where the Spaniards were acting as the American Indians' "saviors," another term easy to manipulate and suit to one's own advantage.

Vitoria's fifth alleged legitimate title was in the defense of the innocent against tyranny. This is the title that speaks of the natives' practice of human sacrifice and cannibalism, referring to them as "tyrannical and oppressive laws."[4] According to Vitoria, it was the Spaniards' moral obligation to interfere in cases such as these, because the "barbarians" should be defended by their fellowmen from such subjugation and cruelty. According to author Yuri Mantilla, the ending of the Indian custom of human sacrifice, a direct violation of natural law and the right to life, was Vitoria's most compelling justification for the use of force by the Spanish in the New World. Again, we see an interesting paradox if we consider that the Spaniards were generally the oppressive, dominating force from which the American Indians needed to be defended. Vitoria here gives the Spaniards a lot of power, to surpass not only the pope's approval but also that of the very people whom they presumably defended. According to Vitoria, this was a "moral" duty of the Spaniards and "it makes no difference that all the barbarians consent to these kinds of rites and sacrifices, or that they refuse to accept the Spaniards as their liberators in the matter" (In Pagden 1991, 288).

"By true and voluntary election" was Vitoria's sixth legitimate reason. Here he also presents a relatively straightforward, although impossibly idealistic, argument: "Imagine the barbarians recognized the wisdom and humanity of the Spaniards' administration. And one and all, both masters and subjects, spontaneously decided to accept the king of Spain as their prince. This could happen and might be a legitimate title under natural law" (In Pagden 1991, 288). Vitoria uses the "majority rules" theory, saying that the majority vote outweighed the minority. That would mean that even if not all the "barbarians" recognized the "wisdom and humanity" of the Spaniards and decided to not accept the king of Spain as their ruler, but *most* of them did, then that would be enough to make it official. If this were not so, for Vitoria, no real effective action could ever be taken for the community, since a unanimous verdict or consensus of ideas would be impossible.

Vitoria's seventh title for legitimate Spanish presence in the New World and a just cause for war at the same time was for the sake of allies and friends. Here, using the authority of Cajetan, he claims that "there can be no doubt that fighting on the behalf of allies and friends is a just cause of war, as Cajetan declares" (In Pagden 1991, 289). For this argument, he uses the specific example of Cortés's alliance with the Tlaxcaltecs against Moctezuma and his Aztec warriors in 1519. The Tlaxcaltecs had been fighting the Aztecs and had made a treaty with Spain for their help in exchange for giving them the spoils of the war.

The eighth and last legitimate title that Vitoria proposes is his most hesitant one and has to do with the mental capacity of the barbarians:

> There is one further title which may be mentioned for the sake of argument, though certainly not asserted with confidence; it may strike some as legitimate, though I myself do not dare to affirm or condemn it out of hand. It is this: these barbarians, though totally not mad, as explained before, are nevertheless so close to being mad, that they are unsuited to setting up or administering a commonwealth both legitimate and ordered in human and civil terms. (In Pagden 1991, 290)

He then proceeds to explain why this may be so, due to the American Indians' lack of many of the essentials of a "civilized commonwealth," again contradicting rather strongly his previous argument on the American Indians' possession of reason and their right to handle and have control over their own private affairs. This is yet another example of a situation that could be easily manipulated by the "higher powers" such as the Crown or church, to fit their own personal interests. Anything could really be proven to be in the American Indians' interest, according to the way it was interpreted. This is yet another example of the contradictory nature of Vitoria's arguments. When discussing illegitimate titles to Spanish domination previously, he had listed all the attributes of the American Indians that fully qualified them as rational men. Here, he is going directly against that position and explicitly refers to the American Indians as children, with the Spaniards acting as their "loving neighbors" and tutors until they reached the "age of reason."

This last part of Vitoria's discussion is heavily riddled with contradictions and at the very end he addresses again the Aristotelian question of natural slavery with which he dealt earlier in the *relectio*, but approaching it from a completely different angle. By now listing what the American Indians *did not* have in common with civilized men rather than what they *did* have in common, he seems to have changed his mind on his previous conclusion that the natives were not natural slaves under any pretext. Vitoria argues that "what was said earlier about some men being natural slaves might be relevant. All these barbarians appear to fall under this heading, and they might be governed partly as slaves" (In Pagden 1991, 291).

In conclusion, Vitoria struggled to answer and solve the imperial doubts and questions regarding the conquest and did so in a more "diplomatic" way, never taking too much power away from authorities or when doing so, making sure that there were so many loopholes and exceptions in the argument that one could easily navigate his way through. He never argued that the Spaniards should *leave* the Indies. He rather attempted to clarify the reasons *why* they should be there and *how* they should behave while there, giving the Spanish sovereigns the power to legitimize themselves. Vitoria argued that majority consent is what gave the *ius gentium* its authority, but how were the Spaniards in the New World considered a majority over the natives of the land? Toy-Fung Tung explains,

> In Amerindian lands, the Spanish were a majority, not as members of any earthly commonwealth, but as members of the mystical Church. . . . As members of the supernatural unity of the mystical Church, Spaniards in the New World could consider themselves authorized by Christ's highest moral law to impose their privileged version of majority order on new lands and peoples conceded human rights but stripped of civil identity. (Tung 2014, 21)

Vitoria actually went to great pains to describe what legitimate reasons the Spaniards had for being there. The main idea was that the Spanish go there to spread the word of Christianity and to teach the American Indians how to better their culture progressively. This focused objective can also be seen in the papal bull Intercetera and in Ginés de Sepúlveda's work, but the drastic difference between them and Vitoria's stand on the subject was the way in which these arguments were made and the authority referred to in each to uphold the argument. Whereas the papal bull and Sepúlveda's stand on the subject advocated the power of the church and the pope over all worldly things, Vitoria's arguments were fundamentally secular, not religious, and it is in this way more than anything else that his ideas reflected and set the path for modern international law. For Vitoria, it was evident that after the process of conversion of the "barbarians" had already started, it would neither be convenient nor logical for the Spanish to abandon completely the administration and governing of these Amerindian territories. He clearly believes that a policy of complete abandonment would not stand a chance in front of the church or Crown or conquistadores for that matter. What Vitoria was aiming to do rather was to put order to a situation over which, in his opinion, the church and Crown had lost control.

It is important to keep in mind that not too long before, the conquest of the Incan Empire had taken place and the senseless, random, and violent crimes committed by Pizarro and his men had become notorious and needed to be addressed to make sure that nothing like that would ever happen again and ruin Spain's reputation in the face of its European competitors, such as the English and the French. The Crown felt the pressure to justify and right the wrongs that the Spanish conquistadors had committed in order for Spain to keep its position as the strongest imperial power, not necessarily out of a true concern for the morality of their actions. Although Vitoria did value the judgment of the "wise and learned," due to the atrocities that were taking place in Peru, he began to question the whole judgment process: "We may readily suppose that, since the affair is in the hands of men both learned and good, everything has been conducted with rectitude and justice. But when we hear subsequently of bloody massacres and of innocent individuals pillaged of their possessions and dominions, there are grounds for doubting the justice of what has been done" (In Pagden 1991, 238).

For Vitoria, a complete stop to the injustices and cruelty that had taken place with the conquest of the New World by the Spaniards was necessary in order to achieve what should have been the true, and only, objective of such a conquest all along: the complete evangelization of the American Indians and the creation of an organized, moral colonial order. However, although he did advocate for a complete stop to unnecessary violence, Vitoria also stated that "I myself have no doubt that force and arms were necessary for the Spaniards to continue in those parts; my fear is that the affair may have gone beyond the permissible bounds of justice and religion" (In Pagden 1991, 286). This illustrates the fact that although Vitoria was not necessarily promoting violence, he also did not think that the Spanish would get very far in their mission without some use of force. His point was that whatever had to be done should be done in moderation. Spain had no obligation to leave the New World but must (ideally) treat the American Indians with respect while there. A global, peaceful world would be one where everyone would be subordinate to the same powers and same values and beliefs as those in the Christian world. Basically, what Vitoria had done was not change the argument itself of the Spaniards being there, but he justified and defined it under the terms of civil and natural laws instead of divine.

The contradictions and inconsistencies in Vitoria's lectures should not overshadow the brilliance of his work and the revolutionary ideas that he introduced at the time. Vitoria's endeavor to find a new perception of man and his place in the world, consistently carried through or not, clearly inspired future generations to develop his ideas and apply them to their own context.

NOTES

1. During the 1500s, John Mair addressed the question of whether dominion came from natural or civil law and he described to his students eight different kinds of dominion: dominion of the blessed, dominion of the damned, original dominion, natural dominion, gratuitous dominion, evangelical dominion, civil dominion, and canonical dominion. Conrad Summenhart, his contemporary, found twenty-three different kinds of dominion! Thankfully, Vitoria's concept of dominion was not so multifaceted.

2. Some of the early missionaries such as Fray Bernardino de Sahagún and Fray Toribio de Benavente, better known as Fray Alonso de Motolinía, also contributed greatly to the postconquest ethnographic literature on native cultures with their works *Historia General de las cosas de Nueva España* and *Historia de los Indios*, respectively. Reports by conquistadors, such as Hernán Cortés and Bernal Díaz del Castillo, were also historically important but not so ethnographically valuable.

3. Although later, when discussing legitimate titles to Spanish conquest, we do see Vitoria's characteristic contradictions to his own arguments resurface when he addresses the question of natural slaves again at the end of his *relectio*.

4. He goes more into detail on the American Indians' "tyrannical laws" in his *relectio* "De usu ciborum, sive emperantia" (On Dietary Laws, or Self-Restraint), where he explains that, "since it is a fact that these barbarians kill innocent men, at least for sacrifice, princes may wage war on them to force them to give up these rituals. Even if they sacrifice criminals to eat, they still commit an injustice (*iniuria*), since there is a law of nations (*ius gentium*), indeed a natural law, that the bodies of the dead are exempt from this injustice" (225).

Chapter 4

Vitoria on Just War and International Law

The morality and justness of war is a concept that has been disputed for many centuries and is still a controversial topic today. Throughout the times, intellectuals have formulated different theories delineating the ethical boundaries of a moral use of force (*jus ad bellum*) as well as the behavior justified in war (*jus in bello*). The different perspectives on war being just in certain conditions and war never being justifiable under any circumstances have kept this issue pertinent and alive to this very day.

Vitoria's *relectio* "De iure belli" (On Just War) was delivered as a lecture in 1539. In it, Vitoria proposes legitimate reasons for the Spanish invasion of the Americas using the traditional just war theory and definition of just war presented by St. Augustine: "The usual definition of just wars is that they are those which avenge injustices, when a nation or city is to be scourged for having failed to punish the wrongdoings of its own people or to restore property which has been unjustly stolen" (In Pagden 1991, 270). Although just war is the specific focus of this *relectio*, Vitoria also mentions it in others. Therefore, this chapter cites Vitoria regarding the just war not only from this *relectio* but from others as well, such as "On Dietary Laws and Self-Restraint" and "On the American Indians," where he also discusses just war at length.

4.1 JUST WAR THEORY

Just war theory delineates when it is morally justifiable to go to war and when not, and also which conditions should be met and behavior should be displayed once the war has begun, primarily to make sure that the use of force remains within its "moral" scope. The paradox of bringing together the terms of war and justice in a single concept is inevitable in this case and by its very nature is what makes the just war doctrine so controversial. Not only that, but if one thinks about it, the theory of a just war is really nothing more than a way to rationalize the act of warfare. War was declared "just" when it appeared that a certain nation or country was the victim, and the opposing party, the enemy. However, this theory has never been fairly tested, because no nation that has been engaged in war has ever admitted to waging an unjust one. In their eyes, they were always acting justly and in self-defense. A standard that has never been equally applied to one's own country cannot count as a fair, just, or equal measure.[1] The attempt to legalize and moralize war on these terms is highly problematic. This controversial theory continues to evolve along with people's understanding of it.

According to the Vitorian just war theory, the only legitimate reasons to go to war were for self-defense, in which case it is lawful to meet force with force and to right a wrong, or any attempt to deprive a man of his natural rights, the avenging of which gave legitimate reason for a just war. The only legitimate goal in a just war was the restoration of peace and justice and in these cases, Vitoria emphasizes that only sufficient force should be used to resist violence and restore peace. The amount of violence and revenge the victors would bestow on the vanquished had to be equal to the injury inflicted by the defeated on their victims and not surpass it.

A just war must also be undertaken with right (moral) intentions in mind. According to St. Augustine, this should always be focused on the "Christian love" for one's neighbors and enemies alike. A just war should never and could never be waged out of hatred or revenge and should really only be started with the idea that good will ultimately result from this use of force. A just society was ruled by justice and reason and these principles were key factors in the declaration and conduct of war. A major premise of a just war is that it be done, ironically enough, out of "Christian love" and for the restoration of peace and civil order.

Vitoria also argues that for a war to be just, it is necessary to analyze well the causes of war and if there is justice in them. The arguments on both sides should be considered if both sides were prepared to negotiate fairly. Of course, in order for this to happen,

> it is necessary to examine the justice and causes of war with great care, and also to listen to the arguments of the opponents, if they are prepared to negotiate genuinely and fairly. As Terence says, "In every endeavor the seemly course for the wise man is to try persuasion before turning to force" (*Eunuchus* 789). One must consult reliable and wise men who can speak with freedom and without anger or hate or greed. (In Pagden 1991, 307)

Once again, we are confronted with Vitoria's unrealistic approach. Obviously, there will be an inevitable bias on each side involved. So who would these impartial, "reliable and wise" men be? What would the requirements be for becoming one of these men? And from where would they get their authority? For Vitoria, the people best fit for this job were the prelates, preachers, confessors, and jurists, who in his opinion were the most learned in divine and human law and would also be the best to determine the legitimacy of a war, having obtained their authority from the king. Vitoria argues that not only were these people the best suited for this task but also it would be impossible to put all that responsibility solely on the shoulders of the king. It is interesting to note here a hint of the more modern idea of popular sovereignty. Vitoria seemed to be rather inclined toward this notion and referred to the majority rule often in his writings.

Another important question to bring up here is whether a war could be just on *both* sides. Vitoria's answer is that this cannot happen except in cases of clear ignorance, because "if it is agreed that both parties have right and justice on their side, they cannot lawfully fight each other, either offensively or defensively" (In Pagden 1991, 313). And what happens when the population is not sure about the justness of a war that they are obliged to support? Vitoria, referring to Augustine's similar argument, states that in these cases the members of the population are obliged to support the war, both defensively and offensively. Then, almost as a way to ease the misgivings of this obligation to participate in a war, even if one was not sure if he supported the cause or not, Vitoria uses Augustine's authority again to smooth things over: "Augustine said plainly that when it is uncertain (that is, unresolved) whether the war is against God's precept, the subject may lawfully fight" (In Pagden 1991, 312). Once again Vitoria demonstrates his skill at manipulating words to convince his readers:

> It is correct to deduce that if I am in doubt as to whether the cause of war is just, I must therefore doubt whether I may lawfully make war or fight in that war. In fact, we must deduce just the opposite: if I am in doubt about the justice of war, it follows that it is lawful for me to go to war at the command of my prince. (In Pagden 1991, 312)

Vitoria also argued for the inevitable use of violence and destruction in a just war in certain situations, "this is particularly the case in wars against the 'infidel,' for whom peace can never be hoped on any terms; therefore the only remedy is to eliminate all of them who are capable of bearing arms against us, given that they are already guilty" (In Pagden 1991, 321). The "infidels" to whom he refers are the Saracens, not the American Indians, but the message is essentially the same: that all means necessary for a victory in war should be permitted.

Vitoria's strongest argument for a Spanish just intervention in the New World rested on the claim that any indigenous resistance to Spanish presence in their territory was a violation of the law of nations, which gave legitimate ground for a just war: "Since these travels of the Spaniards are (as we may for the moment assume) neither harmful nor detrimental to the barbarians, they are lawful" (In Pagden 1991, 278). The first thing that stands out when reading this excerpt from Vitoria's *relectio*, "On the American Indians," is his error in assuming the Spaniards' benevolent intentions. Did he really believe in the pacifist image that he was portraying of the Spaniards? Or was it simply another way of manipulating his words to create a different representation? Vitoria was making the Spaniards seem peaceful when in reality they were not, and he had full knowledge of this, the most specific example being the atrocities in Peru on which Vitoria was well-informed. Overall, Vitoria claims that if the barbarians deny the Spaniards what is theirs by the law of nations, they offend them, which means that the Spaniards may lawfully go to war to obtain their rights. This made it easy for the Spaniards to find a way to claim a just war against the American Indians and, based on these grounds alone, a war against them seemed not only inevitable but limitless.

4.2 "FATHERS" OF THE JUST WAR THEORY

Although the seeds of the idea of a just war doctrine can be traced to the Roman and Greek civilizations, St. Augustine is the one most credited for developing the just war theory, which he primarily based on the ideas of Plato, Aristotle, and Cicero, along with the Scriptures. Plato had argued that states should always be ready to defend themselves against their enemies. Although Plato saw force as an inevitable necessity of politics, he did believe that war should always be conducted within moral limits. Aristotle had also viewed war as an unfortunate but necessary part of life. According to him, war against the barbarians was always just for the latter were intended by nature to be governed by the more civilized and needed to be forcefully brought to submission if they refused to comply with this natural order. Cicero also believed that war was inevitable, but that during war laws should be followed in order to maintain a more humane attitude and not become barbarians themselves.

In the eleventh century, a synod addressing the concept of a just war was held in Charroux, France, and then again at Narbonne. The legislations passed by the bishops during these meetings became part of a peace movement known as The Peace of God and outlined a standard for just behavior during the war (*jus in bello*). Shortly after The Peace of God had been established, bishops convened again and established the Truce of God, which stated approved times when war could be legally conducted.[2] The laws of conduct during war that emerged from these meetings would eventually become officially codified in the church's canon law.

St. Augustine, in his famous work, *The City of God*, addressed the paradox of being a faithful and sincere Christian while still being able to meet the demands of living in a world where violence was somewhat of a necessity. Augustine relied more on moral than legal principles when formulating his concept of a just war and used Cicero's idea of right intention in declaring war. A war needed to comply with three things in order to be considered just: first, it had to have a just cause; second, it had to be declared by a recognized, official authority; and third, it could only be waged with the rightful intention, to preserve civil order and lasting peace. Augustine was concerned more with the dehumanizing effects of war and its negative effect on people than with defining exactly what made a war just. What he most feared about war was that people would come to embrace war and violence with no repercussions.

St. Thomas of Aquinas speaks of just war in Book Two of his *Summa*, where he argues that any decision to resort to war and the use of violence must be strictly focused on justice and the common good. When it comes to the criteria necessary for declaring a just war, Aquinas does not stray far from Augustine's arguments. Just authority, just cause, and just intention were essential standards of a just war, and always with the ultimate objective to establish justice, civil order, and peace. Also similar to Augustine, and later Vitoria, Aquinas believed that war was a necessary evil at times in order to fulfill the responsibilities of protecting the civil population and the church. Just wars done under this pretense for Aquinas displayed Christian love and strong faith, when one was willing to take up the sword in the name of the Lord.

4.3 THE BASIS FOR A JUST WAR

In this *relectio* on just war, Vitoria makes four specific points: first, whether Christians may make war at all; second, where the authority for making war comes from; third, what the causes of just war are; and fourth, which measures may be taken against an enemy and to what extent. In this part of his *relectio* Vitoria strongly demonstrates his opposition to Luther and to the pacifism of the Protestants in general and goes directly against Luther's claim that it is never lawful for Christians to take up arms against other human beings. He uses the ideas of Aquinas, Augustine, and select quotes from the Bible to support his theory that Christians do in fact have a right to wage war for specific (and of course just) reasons. Vitoria explains that since Abraham fought against four kings in the Bible, it was obvious that war was permitted under natural law: "War was permitted under the natural law, as shown by Abraham, who fought against the four kings (Gen. 14: 14-16); it was also permitted in Mosaic Law, as the cases of David and the Maccabees show" (In Pagden 1991, 297). It is also important to note that the question of whether Christians may ever lawfully go to war or not had already been established during the Crusades (sanctified by the church) in the Middle Ages. Throughout this time, there was no question of whether or not Christians could be soldiers and participation in the Crusades was actually seen as a sign of true religious devotion. Anyone who was killed during these Crusades was assured a place in heaven for fighting in the name of the Lord.

Echoing Augustine and Aquinas, Vitoria also argues that "there can be no security for the commonwealth unless its enemies are prevented from injustice by fear of war" (In Pagden 1991, 300). Vitoria's idealism and optimism, so characteristic of his other arguments, are remarkably absent in this case. Here he seems to take the Machiavellian stance that the use of violence to strike fear in the commonwealths' enemies is an absolute necessity for its survival and the repelling of force with force is a part of natural law. This theory of Vitoria is actually more realistic than others in its objectives.

Vitoria does limit the things that need to be addressed by war by claiming that only sins against nature that constituted an injury to humanity itself could provide the basis for a just war. Even though it is obvious that this is another one of Vitoria's arguments that could be manipulated relatively easily to fit other more self-serving objectives, it is important to note that Vitoria did claim that not all sins against nature constituted a reason for just war. However, he does specify that cannibalism and human sacrifice *do* constitute a legitimate reason to go to war, in order to "protect" the innocent, which is the universal "obligation" of neighbors toward one another. This exception to Vitoria's "no war against crimes of nature" rule is explained by him as being perfectly logical because "it follows that the reason why barbarians can be conquered is not that their anthropophagy and human sacrifices are against natural law, but because they involve injustice (*iniuria*) to other men" (In Pagden 1991, 225). Not only that, but the Spaniards in Vitoria's opinion were bound to perform this "civil duty" regardless if the "victims" had asked for help or not. Once this reason has been removed, however, the warfare must come to an end.

4.4 UNJUST REASONS FOR GOING TO WAR

Vitoria presents three unjust reasons for going to war: difference of religion, extension of empire, and the personal glory of the prince. With the difference of religion, Vitoria explains that if the Christian religion is only presented in a certain way to the "barbarians" and they do not accept it, this is by no means an excuse for waging war. Even if the Christian faith is preached to the Amerindians with "provable and rational arguments and accompanied by manners both decent and observant of the law of nature" and they still do not accept it, this is still no reason to go to war against them (In Pagden 1991, 271). Ironically enough, Vitoria praises the freedom of choice supposedly advocated by the Christian religion and says that by forcing unbelievers to the Christian faith, the true Christian objective is obscured: "It has never used force with unbelievers, but always reasoning and proofs. The glorious reputation would be tarnished if we were to start forcing men to accept the law of Christ" (In Pagden 1991, 229). Not surprisingly, however, he soon adds to this argument his customary exceptions and declares that

> if the barbarians, either in person of their masters or as a multitude, obstruct the Spaniards in their free promulgation of the Gospel, the Spaniards, after first reasoning with them to remove any cause of provocation, may preach and work for the conversion of that people even against their own will, and may if necessary take up arms and declare war on them, insofar as this provides the safety and opportunity needed to preach the Gospel. (In Pagden 1991, 285–286)

Even though he is not going *directly* against his argument that war cannot be waged on "infidels" because of their unbelief, he *is* claiming that interfering with or opposing the promulgation of the Christian faith could provide a just cause for war. Here, the paradox becomes evident as he goes from rejecting religion as a just reason to go to war to leaving the door wide open for the Spaniards to do just that and use this to justify future Spanish conquests. The justification of waging war to stop restrictions on the spreading of Christianity also bears a striking resemblance to the Islamic concept of the *jihad*, a "holy war" that persecutes those who impede the spreading of the Islamic faith and culture.

Vitoria also claims that war done for the extension of an empire is unjust, but then justifies the Roman Empire's way of using the law of war to occupy enemy territories. He claims that in this case, war done for the extension of an empire was just since it had been defended by the highest authoritative figures: "The justice and legitimacy of the Roman Empire is defended by Augustine, Jerome, Ambrose, Aquinas and other holy doctors" (In Pagden 1991, 325). This is one of the many loopholes in Vitoria's arguments that become readily apparent as we delve more into his theories.

The third unjust reason to go to war that Vitoria mentions was for the personal glory of the prince. For Vitoria it was obvious that a war should never be waged for the personal interest of the king. This argument of his is very straightforward: "Laws must not be framed for the convenience of any private individual, but for the common utility of the members of the commonwealth" (In Pagden 1991, 303).

4.5 TREATMENT OF THE ENEMY POPULATION AND JUST BEHAVIOR DURING WAR (*JUS IN BELLO*)

Vitoria argues that a war should be waged in moderation, keeping in mind the common good of all involved, including the enemy. However, he then claims that the victors of a just war may take the property of the defeated as their own and the prisoners taken during warfare may be lawfully enslaved. There does not seem to be much moderation or common good in these acts. Here we see again the conflicting nature of many of his arguments. If only sufficient force should be used and everything done in moderation, as he had preached before, how does he then also claim that revenge is not only legitimate but even the victors' right?

Vitoria does claim that it is not lawful to kill the innocent members of the enemy population during war, "even accidentally and unintentionally, except when it advances a just war which cannot be won any other way" (In Pagden 1991, 316). Vitoria argues that not only should innocent members of the enemy population not be killed during war but travelers, visitors, clergy, monks, women, and children should not be harmed under any circumstances. This sounds very sincere, but it soon becomes riddled with his characteristic exceptions. For example, he lists some cases in which the killing of the innocent cannot be avoided and is permissible, for example, as an accidental result of another justified or necessary act of war, such as the storming of an enemy city. He even takes it further: "If the state of war is permanent, it is lawful to plunder the enemy indiscriminately, both innocent and guilty, since the enemy relies upon the resources of its people to sustain an unjust war" (In Pagden 1991, 317). Thus, Vitoria goes from claiming that the innocent should not be harmed unless there is no other way, to saying that it is lawful to plunder them indiscriminately as indirect resource suppliers to the enemy.

This position is radically different from his previous advocacy of moderation and humility and conserving the lives of the innocent. However, he does follow this argument with mitigating circumstances, for example, "If the war can be satisfactorily waged without plundering farmers or other non-combatants, *it is not lawful to plunder them*" (In Pagden 1991, 317). Nonetheless, one still does notice that now the killing of the innocent has gone from only being done when there is no other way around it to being permissible simply if the war is not being satisfactorily carried out. He has also changed from moderation in war to claiming that it is not only lawful but sometimes even necessary to kill all the enemy combatants for a future guarantee that a war against them will never happen again. In this part of the *relectio*, Vitoria appears to be more than ever torn between his Christian conscience and the need to justify his country's actions.

In order to assure the war being just, Vitoria presents the idea of a "court of conscience" in which he assigns the job of "judge" to the victors' king. This is a pretty unrealistic concept, because the judge is supposed to keep the well-being of both parties in mind with no bias:

> The victor must think of himself as a judge sitting in judgment between two commonwealths, one the injured party and the other the offender; he must not pass sentence as the prosecutor, but as a judge. He must give satisfaction to the injured, but as far as possible without causing the utter ruination of the guilty commonwealth. (In Pagden 1991, 327)

However, by establishing this idea of a neutral judge and court during and after a war, Vitoria did lay down the groundwork for moral restraints and ethical guidelines that should be recognized by all, even in the midst of the chaos of war. These principles of moral behavior were a big step in focusing a war on the establishment of a lasting peace. As unrealistic as that may have sounded at that time, in 1899 the Hague Convention followed up on this idea as representatives from different countries met to discuss what exactly constituted just behavior during war and declared bombing of enemy cities unjust, since it involved the massacre of innocent civilians. The question of how noncombatants and prisoners of war should be treated was the main issue at this convention. These meetings eventually made up the world's first "official" international rules of war which were promulgated through the Geneva conventions of 1864, 1906, 1929, 1948, and 1949, and also through peace conferences at The Hague in the Netherlands in 1899 and 1907.

The Hague conferences defined the behavior that should be followed by nations engaging in war, especially the roles and rights of combatants in war. The Geneva conventions were established to protect noncombatants during war and the rights of combatants or prisoners of war who were no longer engaged in warfare. However, considering the use of weapons of mass destruction in modern wars, it is clear that this principle of protecting those not involved directly in the war does not carry a lot of weight and does not seem to be the primary concern for nations when engaging in war. For example, after the Hague Conventions prohibited the use of bombs on enemy cities where innocent civilians lived, in World War II, both sides, the Axis and the Allies, bombed enemy cities and claimed that they had the right to do so due to the fact that every member of the enemy country was a potential risk. This sounds remarkably similar to Vitoria's argument mentioned previously that this could be done "justly" in order to "eliminate any future threat."

4.6 VITORIA'S THREE CONCLUDING POINTS

At the end of this *relectio*, Vitoria states three overarching rules: first, that the prince, even with the authority to wage war, should try above all else to avoid it; second, once a war has been declared the prince should not be concerned with the destruction of his opponents, but rather focus on the pursuit of justice and the defense of his empire; and third, after victory has been obtained, the victors should exercise moderation and humility above all else. However, as mentioned before, let that not fool us into thinking of Vitoria as a peacemaker adverse to violence. Vitoria does also argue that after the war is over, it is lawful to get revenge on the enemy:

> Even after victory has been won and property restored to its rightful owners, and peace and security are established, it is lawful to avenge the injury done by the enemy, and to teach the enemy a lesson by punishing them for the damage they have done . . . the world could not exist unless some men had the power and authority to deter the wicked by force from doing harm to the good and the innocent. (In Pagden 1991, 305)

4.7 VITORIA'S THEORY OF LAW OF NATIONS (JUS GENTIUM) AND "MODERN" JUST WAR

Regardless of the inconsistencies in some of his ideas, Vitoria's most valuable contribution to the modern just war theory has been his idea that the world would be more peaceful if the nations came together to form a type of international community. As McKenna argues, "Vitoria not only defined international law, but he also stated the relationship of states to one another. He visualized an international society constituting one integral political order" (McKenna 1932, 728). This view of an international organization to preserve peace and diffuse crisis by addressing problems that lead to war before has turned into reality in Vitoria's far future, our world today. After the atrocities performed during and after World Wars I and II, world leaders came together to create first the League of Nations and then the United Nations (UN).

At the Treaty of Versailles, in January of 1920, the League of Nations was established. Although the League of Nations was never able to achieve its full potential and its dismemberment is linked perpetually to World War II, it did set the stage for future attempts at establishing a peaceful universal order (UN), and the International Court of Justice has survived. The failure of the League of Nations rested primarily in the fact that it was unable to attract leaders from the United States and maintain the confidence of other world leaders who were already members, because of the possible risk of losing their sovereignty. The UN learned from this and has been able to survive, due to the fact that the large nations of the world were assured that their sovereignty would in no way be minimalized by their membership.

The UN first made its appearance on the international political stage in 1942, when President Franklin Roosevelt spoke of the need of the twenty-six allied nations to come together to solidify their forces against the Axis nations of Germany, Japan, and Italy. After World War II, representatives from fifty countries came together in San Francisco to draft the first Charter of the UN. On October 24, 1945, the United States, France, China, the United Kingdom, the Union of the Soviet Socialist Republics, and several other countries sanctioned the UN Charter and the UN was born. Today, there are 193 countries that are members of the UN and each of them is a member of the UN General Assembly. The UN affirmed the existence of a just war principle and recognized the individual need of a nation to protect and defend itself against aggressors in Article 51 of the UN Charter: "Nothing in the present Charter shall impair the inherent right of individual or collective self-defence if an armed attack occurs against a Member of the United Nations, until the Security Council has taken measures necessary to maintain international peace and security" (UN, *Charter of the United Nations*, 4).

Although the UN cannot be thought of as a world government and definitely lacks the arbitrary force and legitimate executive authority to carry out many of its objectives, it should be recognized nonetheless for its invaluable role as a mediator and crisis-diffuser. The UN is able to provide the world with a universal forum for discussion and debate which in turn leads to the possibility of being able to resolve conflicts without resorting to arms. It also offers nations a public stage on which they express their concerns and share their opinions. Regardless of its beneficial attributes, resistance to the UN is evident in many nations, including the United States, particularly recently. For example, in 2002, President Bush declared that if the UN did not respond to Iraq's threats to the United States in a favorable manner, it ran the risk of irrelevance in the modern world. As Tung describes in his work *Just War Claims: Historical Theory, Abu Ghraib, and Transgressive Rhetoric*,

> Prevalent discussions of just war buttressed the Bush administration's heightened discourse of "secularization" and exceptional moral claims, resulting in a climate conducive to supporting not only the Iraqi invasion (jus ad bellum), but also systematic incursions against all political, legal, moral, and even plainly human, limits on war conduct (jus in bello), as exemplified by the Yemeni missile strike, the Coalition Provisional Authority (CPA), and the Abu Ghraib prison. (Tung 2011, 33)

Another example can be seen in the Trump administration and its relationship with the UN. Recently, in his third speech to the UN General Assembly on September 24, 2019, President Trump reiterated the "America First" theme and advised world leaders to reject globalism and to watch out more for the interests of their own respective countries; "The future does not belong to globalists. The future belongs to patriots. The future belongs to sovereign and independent nations" (NPR). This mindset illustrates an active resistance to the UN and a focus placed more on nationalism than on multilateralism. After the United States' deadly strike against the prominent Iranian general, Qassem Soleimani, President Trump threatened to attack Iranian cultural sites should there be any retaliation for this. Boris Johnson, United Kingdom's prime minister, warned that this action would be a violation of international law, since targeting and destroying cultural sites during a conflict was forbidden under the terms of the Hague Convention, of which the United States is a part. The leaders of the United Kingdom, France, and Germany issued a statement asking the United States to show "the utmost restraint and responsibility" and not engage in a full-out war with Iran. This current crisis has made the relationship between the United States and its European allies tense and has caused the administration of the United States to accuse the UN once again of being unhelpful and obstructive, and question the effectiveness of multinational efforts.

Regardless of the peace-making and -keeping efforts, effective or not, of the UN, in many cases war does seem to be inevitable and has sadly enough become a norm in today's world when addressing conflicts between nations. As Donald A. Wells states, "If men can talk of abolishing war with more war, banishing force with superforce, saving life with bullets, and securing the future with thermonuclear explosions, there may, indeed, be little hope that man can save man from an ultimate Armageddon" (Wells 1967, 60).

4.8 VITORIA'S CONCEPT OF INTERNATIONAL LAW

Although Vitoria did not have a *relectio* dedicated specifically to his concept of international law, he did make references to it in his other *relectios*. He believed that there existed a common human nature, a common humanity, among all people. Therefore, the law of nations was to be arrived at by a process of natural reasoning that all men shared, and a majority consensus would have the force of law even if not everyone was in agreement with it. The law of nature was the source from which the rules of the law of nations were primarily derived, but at the same time, was separate from it. Natural law, as discussed before, is inherent in every person and therefore immediately evident to human reason and independent of human judgment, whereas the law of nations requires the intervention of human analysis and thought to determine whether a certain practice is just or not. As Gaius states in his *Institutes*,

> Every people that is governed by statutes and customs observes partly its own peculiar law and partly the law common to all mankind. That law which a people establishes for itself is peculiar to it, and is called *ius civile* as being the special law of that state, while the law that natural reason establishes among all mankind is followed by all peoples alike, and is called *ius gentium* as being the law observed by all mankind. (Gaius 1904, 6)

In Justinian's *Institutes*, the law of nations is also interpreted as the law common to all humans derived from natural law and human reason, however, there is a slight variation in the way natural law is defined as that which nature has taught all animals rather than just humans. Isidore of Seville had a primary role in the preservation and codification of Gaius's concept of the law of nations. In his *Etymologiae*, Isidore listed the treatment of prisoners during war and peace treaties as belonging also to the law of nations which was applicable to *almost* everyone. The use of the adverb "almost" is a minor but significant modification, because it weakened the association between the law of nations and natural law. For Aquinas, the law of nations was an aspect of human law that was derived from natural law, which was applicable universally across jurisdictions and nations. Although Vitoria does stress the separation between these two realms of law, he also emphasizes that the law of nations plays a vital part in preserving the rights of man under natural law. The law of nations has reason as its fundamental source, but with a changeable content, following the progression and variability of human civilization, whereas natural law is static and unalterable.

In his *relectio*, "On Church Power I," Vitoria describes his concept of the law of nations:

> The law of nations (*ius gentium*) does not have the force merely of pacts or agreements between men, but has the validity of a positive enactment (*lex*). The whole world, which is in a sense a commonwealth, has the power to enact laws which are just and convenient to all men; and these make up the law of nations. . . . No kingdom may choose to ignore this law of nations, because it has the sanction of the whole world. (In Pagden 1991, 40)

This law of nations was created in part out of the differences between dissimilar cultures and the questions and issues that were generated by the encounters between these cultures. Vitoria attempted to create a worldwide system of law that could be used in relations between diverse nations and societies, using Gaius's formulation of the *ius gentium* as that which natural reason had established among all the nations of the world. This Vitorian universal system would bind the Spaniards and American Indians alike by evoking the indisputable authority of natural law, which would create a common framework for these distinct political entities and which would in turn shift the focus of authority from divine law and the pope to natural law and a secular sovereign.

Vitoria's law of nations also carried with it the concept of the more "civilized and fortunate" helping the lesser, which sounds remarkably similar to the idea followed in today's international law. European practices were exemplified as the universal model by which all should abide in order to avoid sanctions and isolations from others and be welcomed into the universal community, again very similar to the international political system of today. Here, one can see an example of Vitoria's "two-sided" American Indian. He first speaks of the American Indians' ability to use reason like the rest of mankind, by which they are automatically considered a part of the universal community, but then describes their differences from the Spaniards and their need for tutoring and guidance before entering the universal community. He believed that the American Indians' social and cultural practices did not quite meet the collective European standard or norms. However, they were not a lost cause due to this. On the contrary, this naive American Indian has the potential to achieve perfection by following the Spanish example. Also used as a way to legitimize the Spanish presence in the New World, Vitoria claims that the Spanish governance of the American Indians was to be specifically for their welfare and education, so that they would be able to learn firsthand how to become "real," civilized human beings and members of the universal community.

Vitoria's strongest point with the law of nations was the right of the Spaniards to travel, trade, and reside in the New World without being harmed or stopped. This basically meant that any defensive act of the American Indians would give the Spaniards grounds for a just war, since it would be a violation of the law of nations. In essence, these imposing norms made the American Indians easy targets. Vitoria argued that majority consent would give the law of nations its authority; the first being the people's consent to a ruler, the second the rulers' consent to each other's authority, and the third the majority's consent.

To get a better idea of how much of Vitoria's ideas found resonance in the writings of his successors, and how this shift from divine law to natural law continued to develop after his time, it is fundamental to take a deeper look at whom some claim to be the "harvester" of Vitoria's ideas: Hugo Grotius. Vitoria's teachings on the New World and Spain's responsabilities there are what founded the modern school of international law, and Grotius, being a member of such school, wrote a treatise that would essentially be a culmination of many of Vitoria's teachings. One planted the seeds of international law's growth and the other cultivated the crops and refined it.

NOTES

1. Charles Montesquieu (1689–1755), for example, argued that war was a legal right which every nation gave to itself and denied to all others.
2. War was outlawed from the start of Advent in the beginning of December until the Octave of the Epiphany in mid-January and from Ash Wednesday in March to the Monday before the Octave of Pentecost at the end of May. Generally, holidays of well-known saints were also counted as "peace" days.

Chapter 5

The Vitorian Concept of Law and Just War in Hugo Grotius

Spain was not the only nation feeling the need to break out of the status quo and question the Christian and—paradoxically—Aristotelian doctrine that was the established canon at the time. I refer to this as paradoxical due to the fact that many of the Christian doctrine's "truths" rested heavily on the theories of a *pagan* philosopher. Other European powers, such as the Dutch and the English, also wanted to reformulate and rearticulate the fundamental ideas of natural law, just war, and human rights. To get a better sense of this overarching phenomenon from a wider perspective, an analysis of the highly influential works of philosophers and theorists such as Hugo Grotius (Hugo de Groot) and John Locke is not only important but absolutely essential.

Hugo Grotius was born in 1583 in Delft, Holland, during the Dutch war of independence from Spain, from an educated and successful family. He was a child prodigy and when he was eleven he became a student of the reputable University of Leiden. At the age of fifteen, he accompanied Johan van Oldenbarnevelt, the prime minister of the Dutch Republic, on an embassy to the king of France, Henry IV. This experience enabled Grotius to get a first-hand view of some of the problems that the new republic was experiencing. Shortly thereafter, the Dutch government called on Grotius to be an intermediary in the dispute between the United Provinces and England over the free access of the seas for all. This would not be the only time that Grotius was called on by the Dutch government to intervene and settle a dispute with a foreign power. He was also asked to intervene in the dispute about the Dutch right to commercial access in Southeast Asia. Grotius had begun as a self-taught lawyer, but his skill and fame as an adviser was developing and along with that, his political influence.

Grotius's work, *De Jure Belli ac Pacis* (*On the Law of War and Peace*), published in 1625, when much of Europe was in turmoil and dealing at length with the concept of a just war, is an extension of his prior work, *De Jure Praedae* (*Commentary on the Law of Prize and Booty*), written in 1604–1605 but not published until 1868. Chapter twelve of this work was published separately in 1609 as *Mare Liberum* (*The Freedom of the Seas*). This was the document that Grotius wrote in light of the dispute with the Portuguese about private possession of the sea. It was published anonymously, probably because, as Grotius himself described, "It seemed to me to be safe, like a painter skulking behind his easel, to find out the judgment of others and to consider more carefully anything that might be published to the contrary" (Grotius 2009, 78). This work was seen by the English and Scots as an attack on their fishing rights in the North Sea and by the Spanish as an overall criticism of the way they had formed their overseas empire. This book had implications for coastal waters and the high seas, for the East and West Indies, and for relations between European and non-European people. Many of the ideas in this work were to be further advanced in *On the Law of War and Peace*, particularly the right of a state to trade with another and the legitimate use of violence to defend this right. These justifications were based heavily on the natural law theory of Francisco de Vitoria.

5.1 THE DISPUTE OVER *STA. CATARINA*

The dispute that proved Grotius's worth as a politician and gained him the most fame began with the question over the legitimacy of the Dutch seizure of a Portuguese ship, *Sta. Catarina*, in the Straits of Singapore in February 1603. Grotius, who at that time was twenty-one years old, was asked to write up a defense of the Dutch East India Company's seizure of the Portuguese ship, claimed by the Dutch to be taken as legitimate booty in a just war. Interestingly enough, Grotius's family participated and had a place in the Dutch East India Company, which had been formed in 1602 through a union of various smaller companies. The Dutch East India Company was one of the first conglomerated big corporations that dominated European overseas expansion in the seventeenth and eighteenth centuries and the De Groots—Grotius's family—were shareholders in the company. Relatives of Grotius had also taken part in the struggle of the northern provinces of the Netherlands to gain independence from the Spanish Crown. Grotius's strong sense of patriotism had some of its foundations here.

Grotius justified the Dutch seizure of the *Sta. Catarina* on the grounds of a set of natural laws that derived from divine law. He argued for the Dutch's right to self-defense and self-preservation as the main reason why the Portuguese ship was seized. He claimed that the Portuguese had been doing evil things to the Dutch and for that reason, Captain van Heemskerck had engaged in a just war against them, out of self-defense, which in turn meant that the spoils taken during such a just battle would be legitimate. Grotius never claimed that the Dutch owned that part of the seas of the East Indies. He is most known for his argument that the seas were open to all equally. Addressing the issue of property over water, Grotius uses a quote from Ovid's *Metamorphoses*: "*Quid prohibetis aquas? Usus communis aquarum est. Nec solem proprium natura, nec aera fecit, nec tenues undas: in publica munera veni*"—"Why do you deny me water? The enjoyment of water is a common right. Nature has not made the sun private to any, nor the air, nor soft water: the common right I seek" (Grotius 2009, 25). This idea was highly favorable with most scholars and historians and ended up becoming part of international law today.

5.2 UNIVERSAL FREEDOM OF NAVIGATION AND TRADE

Grotius, similar to Vitoria, based a great part of his argument on the theory that there existed by natural law a universal freedom of navigation and trade. For Grotius, communities were protected by the rule of hospitality, which for him was a moral obligation. According to natural law theorist Annabel Brett, the problem with this was that the hospitality that Grotius advocated allowed any community to move around and set up their own "imperium" wherever they chose. Regardless, Grotius argued that the openness and freedom of the seas was a crucial factor in the spread of communication among the different people and nations of the world. It was humanly impossible for a nation or individual to possess any part of the ocean, due to its vastness, constant fluctuation, and lack of fixed boundaries.[1]

With regard to free trade, according to Grotius, it was against the law of nations not only for the indigenous not to allow the Dutch or others to trade with them but also for anyone else to interfere in the open trade. Thus, he also considered it unlawful for "the Portugals," whom he describes as robbers and thieves throughout this work, to attempt to stop the trading of the Dutch with the indigenous. Grotius breaks down the Portuguese claim to the East Indies into three different parts: the rights of possession, navigation, and trade. According to him, the Portuguese had no right of possession based on discovery, because the East Indies had already been inhabited by the indigenous. Similar to Vitoria, Grotius explains that "no man is lord of that thing which neither he himself ever possessed nor any other in his name. These islands we speak of have, and always had, their kings, their commonwealths, their laws and their liberties" (Grotius 2009, 13). For him, the fact that they were unbelievers did not take away their natural right of dominion. Grotius makes sure to refer also to the authoritative figures of St. Thomas Aquinas and the conclusions drawn from the Council of Toledo among others to solidify this argument:

> This is the conclusion both of Thomas and the Council of Toledo, and Gregory and the divines and canonists and almost all the civilians: although faith be declared to the barbarians . . . probably and sufficiently and they will not respect it, yet notwithstanding it is not lawful for this reason to pursue them with wars and spoil them of their goods. (Grotius 2009, 18)

It is interesting to note that Grotius leaves open the possibility of believing in more than one god. He explains that "there is a Deity (one or more I shall not now consider) and that this Deity has the Care of human Affairs, are Notions universally received, and are absolutely necessary to the Essence of any Religion, whether true or false" (Grotius 1949, vol. 2, 1035). This is similar, in a religious sense, to his idea that tyranny would be better than anarchy: "None, even of People the most unpolite and uncivilized, did ever sink so low as to entertain and profess Atheism, but that a Divinity, and a Providence, were allowed and affirmed by all" (Grotius 1949, 1036). Although Grotius seems to respect differences of religion and argues that all are entitled to believe what they choose and cannot be punished for this, nor forcibly converted, he does display a clear preference for the Christian religion by expressing that even though people are to do well to others regardless, special preference should be given to fellow Christians. Grotius makes an excellent point in stating that nobody should be compelled to do or believe what somebody else tells them and are free to make their own choices, "for the Choice of what is profitable or not profitable, where People enjoy their Senses and their Reason, is to be left to themselves" (Grotius 1949, vol. 2, 1106).

Also similar to Vitoria, Grotius argued that the indigenous peoples were not insensible; they did possess reason, and therefore could not be deprived of their possessions according to that title: "Victoria therefore rightly saith that . . . Nor truly are the Amerindians out of their wits and insensible but ingenious and sharp-witted, so that no pretence of subjecting them may be taken from hence" (Grotius 2009, 15). Grotius, like Vitoria, also argues that the pope is not a civil or temporal lord over the world and has no authority over the American Indians: "Whence it followeth, by the opinion of Cajetanus and Victoria and the better part as well divines as canonists, that it is not a sufficient title against the Amerindians" (Grotius 2009, 17).

5.3 RIGHTS OVER THE SEAS

Having dismantled the Portuguese titles to possession of the East Indies, Grotius then begins to deconstruct the Portuguese theories on the rights of exclusive navigation and commerce. Here is where Grotius's argument shifts from the rights over land to the rights over the seas, comparing and contrasting the two. His ultimate objective was to show that the sea could not be private property due to several factors. First, since dominion did rest on physical occupation, it could not apply to a body of water, since one could not physically possess it or do labor on it, due to its fluctuating nature.[2] This was different from the land, which could be physically appropriated and worked.

Grotius maintained that the right of navigation and trade was an essential part of the law of nations and open to all. One of Grotius's key arguments here was that the freedom of the seas did come not only from nature but also from human consent and custom. He argued that God himself created the world with the intention of nature providing many things for man's common use. This freedom of being able to go from one country to another unharmed as long as the rules of that country were followed also applied to exiles, which is particularly interesting due to the fact that Grotius himself was an exile, having fled prison and escaping to France.

5.4 NATURAL LAW

For Grotius, natural law was the one thing that stayed constant and was equal to all. Grotius's view on natural law, similar to Vitoria and later Locke, was that it was inherent in all human beings, regardless of religion or beliefs. Natural law was a perceptive judgment in which things were seen and valued as good or bad by their basic nature and not necessarily through God's revelation. He did not think that one needed to know about God and his divine creation in order to have a sense and knowledge of natural law, since the truth and validity of nature did not depend on God. This was clear, because all kinds of people throughout history, irrespective of their religious beliefs, had agreed on the fundamental principle of natural law: self-preservation. Not even God could change the law of nature: "The Law of Nature is so unalterable, that God himself cannot change it" (Grotius 1949, vol. 1, 155). Although he was by no means an atheist and actually does refer to biblical sources in his writings on several occasions, his intention was to write about law disconnected from religion and religious revelation and keep natural law and divine law separate, even though he does describe divine law as the most perfect law. Grotius also recognized the connection between natural law and the law of nations, but not as strongly as some of his predecessors. He did not disagree with the fact that natural law should be the basis for relations among different states, but he did emphasize that the law of nations, like all human law, was the product of human will.

For Grotius, it was important to maintain church and state powers separated but that this attempt would be futile if the new republic was still controlled by the intolerant Calvinist Church. Grotius worked to protect liberal theologians from the scrutiny and censorship of the Calvinists. In 1611 he wrote *Meletius sive De iis quae inter Christianos conveniunt epistola*, in which he advocated a minimalist version of Christianity. This is where his remarkable background really becomes fascinating. He had basically argued that the only way for the new republic to gain freedom from an oppressive church and gain religious toleration was by mounting a military coup against the Calvinists. Prince Maurice had Grotius arrested for this under the suspicion of heresy and he was sentenced to life imprisonment in the Louvestein Castle in the south of the United Provinces. He was taken there in 1618 and stayed until 1621, when he made his great escape in a both romantic and humorous way. His wife arrived at the castle with a basket of books. The books were then taken out of the basket and Grotius, who was a very small man, hid in the basket where the books had been. This escape plan was a triumph and he went to France, where he ended up living most of his life. Grotius did return to the United Provinces on a few occasions: once under a false identity, since his conviction had in fact never been lifted. He died after being rescued from a shipwreck on August 28, 1645. Ironically, he was given a very honorable burial by the same Dutch authorities who had kept him in exile for more than two decades.

According to Grotius, the two main laws of nature by which everything else was bound were self-preservation and self-defense. Self-preservation included obtaining and keeping anything useful for survival and for life, a natural right that all human beings possessed equally. These two primary laws of nature had boundaries set on them by secondary laws: not to harm anyone without reason and not to seize the possession of others. In Grotius's opinion, the attempts that had been made to place laws into orderly categories had not succeeded, because they had not placed human laws on a drastically different footing from natural laws, which was essential since human laws were constantly changing, whereas natural law always stayed the same. He did remain optimistic however, and did not think that finding a solution to this was impossible.

5.5 *DE JURE BELLI AC PACIS* (*ON THE LAW OF WAR AND PEACE*)

Grotius's work, *De Jure Belli ac Pacis* (*On the Law of War and Peace*), offers the reader an in-depth analysis of his views on war: just, private, and public.[3] He emphasizes the need he felt to write about this topic early on in his work: "I thought this Undertaking still the more worth my Pains, because, as I said before, this Subject has not been fully handled by any Body; and those who have treated of the Parts of it, have done it so, that they have left a great deal for the Labour of others" (Grotius 1949, vol. 1, 108).

Grotius's quest for the "absolute truth" was so important to him that instead of just focusing on a certain, limited number of sources for his work, he used different kinds of sources in juxtaposition with each other to get a better overall idea. Presented in three volumes, *De Jure Belli ac Pacis* is an extensive work that examines every question that could possibly have to do with war. He addresses this issue thoroughly, to say the least, and presents his ideas systematically, making it easy to follow his line of thought and the formulation of his arguments. As he himself explains, "In this whole Work there were three Things that I chiefly proposed to myself; to render the Reasons of my Decisions as evident as possible, to dispose the Matters to be treated of into a regular Method, and to distinguish clearly those Things which might appear to be the same but were not" (Grotius 1949, vol. 1, 131). The clarity of his work was so important to Grotius that he discarded the use of intellectual jargon in favor of a more universal and straightforward language, leaving it up to others to interpret his basic principles or expand on them as they saw fit. The book appeared in Paris in 1625 and immediately incited controversy among Catholics, primarily because Grotius had not referred to the popes by their Roman Catholic titles. *De Jure Belli ac Pacis* was placed on the Papal Index in 1626 and remained here until 1901.

The first volume covers the question of whether any war can be just and explains the difference between a public and a private war, the extent of supreme power, and the obligation subjects have toward their king. The second addresses the causes for a just war to take place. Grotius discusses which things are common among all people, what right a person can have over another, property rights, and other matters. Justifiable causes of war included those that were done for defense, for the recovery of property, or as a punishment for a wrong committed. His general underlying theory when it came to the question of war, albeit riddled with many exceptions, was that "there is no other *reasonable* Cause of making War, but an *Injury* received" (Emphasis in original) (Grotius 1949, vol. 2, 393). The third volume covers what is lawful in war and here Grotius speaks of different forms and levels of violence and punishments. A punishment of death should be avoided but is not unlawful. He describes punishment as "*the Evil that we suffer for the Evil that we do*" (Emphasis in original) (Grotius 1949, vol. 2, 949).

Since self-defense was the most fundamental part of natural law, he claimed that everyone had this right no matter what the circumstances, because ultimately unjust acts against another were violent transgressions of natural law provisions. Nevertheless, this self-defense should only be used for that specific purpose and not to extract revenge, which is contrary to all of God's teachings and against the law of nature. Grotius's belief in the right to self-preservation varies in degrees according to whether it is done in a private war or a public one. The preference for nonviolence that Grotius displays at times in his work, as is illustrated in his ideas on the Christian Laws of Charity, is not sustained throughout all of this treatise. In fact, when it comes to the question of what is allowable in a just war, Grotius's position on violent means shifts. He begins by claiming that "when War is proclaimed against a Nation, it is at the same Time proclaimed against all of that Nation," meaning the people as well (Grotius 1949, vol. 3, 1281). And he means the *entire* populace, including women and children: "The Slaughter of Infants and Women is allowed, and included by the Right of War" (Grotius 1949, vol. 3, 1283). During war, it is lawful not only to kill the enemy but also to take away or destroy his goods and property. His opinion on what is allowable during a period of war seems to stem from the fundamental idea that in a war all things necessary to the end (obtaining just rights and peace) are considered lawful, for the greater good of course.

Nonetheless, Grotius did not necessarily *advocate* violence and he did soften up those statements that seemed to allow unlimited violence by also arguing for leniency and charity and suggesting that although the violence done during war was not unlawful, it should only be done in times of extreme necessity: "*By the Laws of War, only those that are in Arms, and do resist, are to be killed*... but the Innocent should not be touched" (Emphasis in original) (Grotius 1949, vol. 3, 1443). He also displays this more compassionate point of view in the question of how to treat prisoners of war. Again, even though it is lawful to kill enemy prisoners, Grotius explains that mercy should be shown above all. In this respect, he also claims that even though the killing of women of the enemy was lawful, violating them, although not necessarily declared unlawful, was not ethical.

Grotius makes a very interesting point in his work concerning moderation when it comes to the rulers of the vanquished: "There is another Kind of Moderation in Victory, to leave to the Conquered, either Kings or People their own Government" (Grotius 1949, vol. 3, 1501). This point of view cannot be attributed to his compassion but rather to his view of a logical and beneficial outcome: it would be less stress on the victorious empire and would cause less resentment from the defeated at the same time. Grotius here seems to understand the need that the overpowered felt to keep a hold onto some of their own identity. The importance of doing this to keep them pacified and to avoid a bigger catastrophe such as a large-scale rebellion was obvious. In regards to the religion of the defeated, Grotius also made clear that they should be allowed to exercise whatever religion they desired even if that choice was not Christianity. In actuality, the rights and privileges he allots to the subjugated in this treatise are quite remarkable.

Although he was not against war, Grotius did argue that if there was a way to solve disputes without having to resort to it, then that should always be the course of action taken first. For example, even if the victorious party is not reimbursed as much as they are due but are able to come to peaceful terms with the offending party, they should do so without a moment's hesitation, peace being the ultimate objective above all else. There are three ways that Grotius proposes to settle disputes without resorting to war. The first one is by a conference and negotiation among the conflicting parties discussing the issues at hand and coming to a common agreement. The second way is by putting the matter to arbitration with a neutral person acting as the mediator and coming to a compromise between the two parties. The third way is by "casting lots," or dueling. Grotius sees the latter as the lesser evil as compared to war and refers to it as "a Custom which is not altogether to be rejected, if two Antagonists, whose Disputes would otherwise involve whole Nations in Misery and Ruin, are willing to decide the Matter themselves by Sword" (Grotius 1949, vol. 2, 1128). It was only if none of these methods worked that the opposing parties or nations should resort to war. When this happens, Grotius argues strongly that any declaration of war must be declared publicly and not kept secret. Not only should things be acknowledged publicly, but they must be comprehensible and truthful.

Grotius discusses his concept of just versus unjust and how these apply in wartime situations. Addressing the question as to whether or not a war can be lawful on both sides, he reaches a much clearer conclusion than Vitoria: "In the particular Acceptation of the Word, and as it regards the Action itself, War cannot be just on both Sides, nor can any Law Suit be so, because the very Nature of the Thing does not permit one to have a moral Power, or true Right, to two contrary Things" (Grotius 1949, vol. 2, 1130).

In discussing whether or not it is lawful to wage war at all, Grotius relies almost entirely on the Bible to argue his point that war is lawful in certain occasions. He uses numerous examples, such as Abraham, Sodom, Moses, and the Israelites to support his claim. Although he does state that no war should be undertaken but for the obtaining of a right and in that case, display moderation in everything, one finds when reading this treatise that, similar to Vitoria's concepts, these "bounds of justice and fidelity" are open to manipulation and distortion and the lawful possibilities for war can actually be quite numerous.

According to Grotius, one should obey God rather than man, so if one is given orders to fight in what he believes to be an unlawful and unnecessary war, they need not do so. This is contradictory to Vitoria, who argued that even if one was not fully certain that the war was just or not, he should still support the prince. Grotius, on the other hand, reassured those who may be scared of disobeying the prince: "Disobedience in such Cases is in its own

Nature a less Evil than Homicide, especially than taking away the Lives of many innocent People" (Grotius 1949, vol. 2, 1177). Here, Grotius also discusses the disgust he feels toward mercenary soldiers who fight a war without ever questioning the cause, solely for the money, and never questioning the justice of what they are doing.

Grotius does acknowledge the position of those who argued that Christians should not go to war under any circumstances and points out how unrealistic this concept was because Christians had done things that proved to be "shameful even among barbarians . . . they were capable of any crime" (Grotius 1949, vol. 3, 1753). In his opinion, it was clear that war was definitely not against natural law. His argument about the lawfulness of war, broken down to its most simplistic component, was that it was lawful to repel force by force, regardless of religion and belief. This is comparable to our modern-day concept of the lawfulness of killing someone in self-defense (justifiable homicide).

5.6 THREE DIFFERENT TYPES OF WAR

Grotius points out three different types of war: private, public, and mixed. A public war is made on each side under civil power. Private war is one that is made between private individuals, without public authority. Mixed war is one which is made on one side by an official authority and on the other by individuals. According to Grotius, two things are needed for a public war to be lawful: that it be declared by both sides and that it be made official. Private war was legitimate and could even be done by the East India Company if it so chose. In these private wars, Grotius did not really seem to concern himself too much with the limitation of violence or minimizing it to simple self-defense. In Grotius's concept of a private war, individuals or companies had the right to make judgments about the morality and actions of the offending parties and punish those who seemed to be violating others' rights in whichever way they deemed most appropriate according to the injury received. He gives the individuals or companies a lot of intervention power and reminds his readers that the punishment of sins is something that should be dealt with more leniently than other injuries to natural law. He breaks away from the ethical perspective that permeates Vitoria's work and takes a more realistic, Machiavellian approach to the question of punishment for sins committed against natural law. He claims that as human beings "we lie under a Kind of Necessity in general to Sin," and for that reason "there are likewise some Sins, that are not absolutely unavoidable to human Nature" (Grotius 1949, vol. 2, 994). However, not all sins were to be met with this understanding. There were some sins against nature, such as cannibalism, that did require severe punishment. Grotius does conclude, however, that even though undertaking a war for punishment is lawful, in most cases this is an unnecessary and therefore unjust measure.

There is a pretty significant difference between Grotius's concept of love thy neighbor and that of Vitoria. Vitoria claimed, as we have seen, that this was the one rule by which all should live. I have already pointed out the unrealistic and idealistic nature of Vitoria's point of view. Grotius, however, puts the concept in a more practical and realistic light:

> It seems to me more reasonable, that we are not obliged to such a Patience; for we are commanded in the Gospel to love our Neighbours as ourselves, not before ourselves; nay, when an equal Danger threatens us, we are not forbid to take Care of ourselves before others; as we have already shown from the Authority of St. Paul, explaining the Rule of Beneficence. (Grotius 1949, vol. 1, 243–244)

As we can see, it was a duty of mankind to love and respect their neighbors, but that obligation was still superseded by the inherent right of self-preservation.

5.7 NATURE OF A STATE

De Jure Belli ac Pacis also illustrates Grotius's idea of the nature of a state. Like Vitoria, he believed that all the power of the state came from the population, which had invested that power in the state for reasons of self-preservation through the protection of the state. This power came out of a collective agreement, individuals acting as a unit. He referred to the state as a "body" of free persons who came together for a common benefit to be able to enjoy their rights peacefully, very similar to Vitoria's, and later Locke's, ideas of the state and where it got its power. In Grotius's opinion, the human natural instinct for society is also the source of law and the structure and body of the state is completely dissolved when the population itself is no longer together. This would lead to the utter dismantlement of the state and the rights that the subjects had once enjoyed under it would be completely destroyed as well. Grotius's presentation of the majority rule would later be repeated in Locke's idea of a social contract where he voices the necessity of looking at the bigger picture at hand, the greater good, and that God was not necessary for this unification to take place: "That Subjection which we spoke of, began first for the sake of some Advantage . . . Men did not at first unite themselves in Civil Society by any special Command from GOD, but of their own free Will, out of a Sense of the Inability of separate Families to repel Violence" (Grotius 1949, vol. 1, 358). For him, God inscribed his principles in nature and then completely left it up to mankind to make use and reason out of it. Vitoria, Grotius, and Locke all describe the state as a type of body whose parts all need to work together for it to function properly.

Vitoria had argued that the ultimate power always rests with the people and this way there exists a system of checks and balances that the people can use in their favor if their king or other governing power should act malignantly to the health of the state, an idea that would later be repeated by Locke. Grotius, however, strongly disagrees with this:

> We must first reject their Opinion, who will have the Supreme Power to be always, and without Exception, in the People; so that they may restrain or punish their Kings, as often as they abuse their Power. What Mischiefs this Opinion has occasioned, and may yet occasion, if once the Minds of people are fully possessed with it, every wise Man sees. (Grotius 1949, vol. 1, 261)

However, Grotius does later somewhat begrudgingly admit that in some cases a certain system of checks and balances is necessary, and states that there should be restrictions and checks assigned to each party, to make sure that they are following their objectives.

It is clear that for Grotius the order and organization that a government creates and maintains is far more important and valuable than the right of resistance. For this he quotes Barclay, to whom Locke has referred often in his treatise as well, and St. Paul: "He that resists the Power, resists the Ordinance of God, and they that resist, shall receive unto themselves Damnation" (Grotius 1949, vol. 1, 344). He agrees with Vitoria that anarchy is the worst evil imaginable for a state and will surely guarantee its dismantlement and downfall; therefore, to put up with a tyrant's or usurper's laws is at times necessary in order to divert the greater evil. Of course, he does concede that in times of necessity, when there is no other choice left for the survival of the greater good, this prohibition could be lifted.

Grotius does not specify a form of government that he deems best. Similar to Vitoria, he keeps an open mind and argues that it is not so much the form of a government that determines its value, but rather the way in which the governing power is used. Grotius addresses the law of nations and the idea of a universal community voiced so frequently in Vitoria's writings. Similar to Vitoria, he believed that the law of nations depended primarily on majority rule and universal consent. He defines international law as "some Laws agreed on by common Consent, which respect the Advantage not of one Body in particular, but of all in general. And this is what is called the Law of Nations" (Grotius 1949, vol. 1, 94). Any nation that was not willing to be a member of this universal community or abide by the law of nations would then pay the price: "A nation which violates the laws of nature and nations will have renounced its right (*rescindit munimenta*) subsequently to live in peace" (Grotius 1949, vol. 3, 1750). The logic of the law of nations was so obvious that he saw no reason why a nation would not want to be part of its own good.

Although one could say that Grotius was conservative in some of his views, his humanist conception of law and the legal system marks him as a forerunner of modern international law notions.[4] Grotius's concept of natural law had an enormous influence on the philosophical and theological debates taking place during the seventeenth and eighteenth centuries, and he succeeded in extensively developing a concept of moderation in warfare and the idea of prevailing justice among nations. He attempted to harmonize natural and human law and by doing so, was able to develop a framework that was applicable to all nations. His theories as well as those of Vitoria on war and the law of nature continue to be echoed in the works of "liberal" and "modern" philosophers such as John Locke in his *Two Treatises on Civil Government*, which will be discussed in the next chapter.

NOTES

1. Although the sea is common to all, Grotius does explain that what one obtains from the sea becomes his privately.
2. Similar to Locke, discussed in the next chapter, Grotius argued that it was through physical labor and appropriation that one acquired ownership. Locke's concept of property rights is influenced by Grotius, who claimed that "there are some Things which are ours by virtue of a Right *common* to all men; and others which are so by a *particular* Right" (Emphasis in original). For Grotius, and later for Locke, God has given this earth to all mankind in general and at the beginning, there were no disputes over land, because there was enough for all. The introduction of money, surplus, man's greed, and the evolution of mankind, in general, was what led to the demise of this basic concept.
3. Grotius took the title *De Jure Belli ac Pacis* from a phrase in Cicero's *Oratio pro Balbo*.
4. For a closer look at the debate regarding Grotius as the father of international law, see Charles S. Edwards, *Hugo Grotius, The Miracle of Holland: A Study in Political and Legal Thought*, and Ben Kingsbury, *Grotius, Law, and Moral Skepticism: Theory and Practice in the Thought of Hedley Bull.*

Chapter 6

John Locke and the Enlightened Evolution of Vitorian Thought

John Locke was a British philosopher born in the Somerset village of Wrington in 1632. He received his education from the prominent Westminster school and attended the University of Oxford in 1652, where his early scholarly focus was on the classics, although later he also studied medicine and experimental science. He obtained a senior studentship at Christ Church, Oxford, in 1659. A chance encounter with a politician named Lord Anthony Ashley Cooper, whom he treated as a patient in 1666 and with whom he would become very close friends, would greatly affect Locke's life. Lord Anthony Ashley Cooper became the first Earl of Shaftesbury and helped Locke to become a prominent government official. Lord Ashley believed that England would prosper greatly through trade and that the colonies were crucial in this aspect. He convinced King Charles II to create a Board of Trade and Plantations that would gather information about trade and the colonies, with Locke as its secretary.

Locke gained much recognition from his revolutionary writings, which became especially influential during the Glorious Revolution of 1688. He became known by many as one of the founders of a liberal political philosophy that advocated for individual human rights and limited government, the philosophy on which modern-day Western political systems and the American Constitution are based. Although diverse in content, most of Locke's work can be characterized by a strong opposition to authoritarianism on both the individual and governmental levels. With regard to the former, Locke encourages each individual to use reason in searching for the truth, rather than simply accepting the opinion of authoritative figures or believing in superstition. On the governmental level, it is crucial to make a clear distinction between legitimate and illegitimate use of power by institutions. The pursuit of the truth and the use of reason could determine the legitimate functions of institutions and would greatly serve to benefit the well-being of both the individual and society.

In his intriguing *An Essay concerning Human Understanding*, Locke tries to define what the limits of human understanding are. He argues that we can only know the appearance of a thing, of a natural entity, rather than the underlying realties that make up that appearance. Although this work and others, such as *The Reasonableness of Christianity*, *Some Thoughts Concerning Education*, and *A Letters Concerning Toleration*, where he argues for the separation of church and state, were considered groundbreaking and innovative for his time, none had as great an impact as his *Second Treatise of Civil Government*, published in 1690. Here is where he uses natural law to establish his liberal political philosophy. Since this work is also the most relevant for my focus on Vitoria's ideas on natural law, it will be the main focus of this chapter.

6.1 LOCKE'S CONTRACTUAL THEORY OF GOVERNMENT

In his *Second Treatise of Civil Government*, Locke refutes the doctrine of the divine and absolute right of the monarch, an argument made by Sir Robert Filmer in his *Patriarcha*, and, similar to Vitoria, asserts that the sovereignty rests in the people rather than in rulers or the state.[1] Locke introduces a contractual theory of government, where civil societies are formed only when the people choose rulers whom they trust to advance and respect their contract with society. The government derives its authority and power from the consent of the governed. Locke believed that individuals had inalienable rights to life, liberty, and property, and if the situation called for it, they could even replace rulers who failed to protect these. People possessed their natural rights before entering into a civil government and everyone possessed them equally.

Locke was aware of the negative reaction that his words might trigger in those who believed that he was promoting an uprising. Prepared for the opponents he knew he would have to this idea, he argued for its logical nature, using the example of pirates and robbers:

> If they who say it lays a foundation for rebellion, mean that it may occasion Civil Wars, or Intestine Broils, to tell the People they are absolved from Obedience . . . They may as well say upon the same ground, that honest Men may not oppose Robbers or Pirates, because this may occasion disorder or bloodshed. (Locke 1966, 416–417)

Although one cannot label Locke as an instigator of rebellion, he does argue that insurgence is justifiable in some cases. However, later, assuaging the fear of the idea of a rebellion in some of his readers, he assured that they did not need to worry, since "the People, who are more disposed to suffer than right themselves by Resistance, are not apt to stir" (Locke 1966, 418). It becomes obvious that in Locke's opinion this aversion to change and the fear of the unknown and possible dangers were major obstacles in the path of effective and beneficial governmental reform.

Locke's view of the state of nature is one to which all men belong prior to *voluntarily* entering into a society. This state of nature, however, needs a civil government but defines what the task and purpose of a civil government must be. All men are born free and equal in the state of nature, which is one of peace, mutual assistance, and preservation. This obligation of mutual respect, sounding very Vitorian, is inherent in every person: "The state of nature has a law of nature to govern it, which obliges every one; And reason, which is that Law, teaches all mankind, who will but consult it, that being all equal and independent, no one ought to harm another in his life, health, liberty, or possessions" (Locke 1966, 271). Locke argues that universal preservation is the fundamental purpose of natural law and that God gave people society as a protective force to help ensure their survival and as a way for them to enjoy the gifts of language and reason with which he endowed them.

Locke and Vitoria voice similar ideas on the natural need for companionship found in humans; however, for Vitoria the urgency and obligation for mankind to become part of a society/commonwealth was much greater than that expressed by Locke. As I have pointed out in the previous chapters concerning Vitoria, this obligation of neighborly love is overly idealistic. In *Civilization and Its Discontents*, Freud conveys his impression of this supposed mutual obligation among humans and describes it as an immoral authoritative order concocted by civilization and society to have more control over mankind and its naturally aggressive human instinct. Society is the controlling force that unites individuals by using the threats posed by nature and by themselves, in order to drive them to form groups and societies and curb their natural instincts. Freud argues that because of this repression of instinct, civilization is built on the denial of what man really is. This constitutes a paradox and makes the essence of society and that of the individual stand in opposition to one another. Locke also argues against the idea that mankind would not be able to survive in the state of nature. He contradicts those, such as Richard Hooker, who affirm that there never existed men in the state of nature because man is incompetent to fend for himself and needs others to survive. Locke states that all men are naturally in that state and remain there until they themselves decide to become a part of society. He also emphasizes, however, that even if one gives up his existence in the state of nature when entering into a contract with society, he is not giving up his freedom but acquires a different type of freedom, the "Freedom of Men under Government."

6.2 FREEDOM AND LIBERTY

Locke makes a clear distinction between freedom and liberty. Freedom is inherent in each individual from the beginning, with or without law, whereas liberty can only be attained under law. In order to become part of a society, a person had to do more than give up his freedom found in the state of nature: he actually had to make a specific contract with the government, an official declaration of his consent to become a member of the commonwealth. Interestingly enough, not only could foreigners become members of a commonwealth provided that they made a declaration of the desire to do so, but Locke also exempts them from the laws of whatever country they are visiting, since they were not under any society's laws other than their own. This concept of impunity is still applied in our present day to the representatives of foreign governments in another country, who are protected from prosecution by the local authorities by diplomatic immunity. Locke also addresses the question of naturalization and says that a father cannot pass on his citizenship of a country to his offspring. To solidify this point, Locke uses what seems to be his fundamental argument for the majority of his ideas: "*Every Man* being, as has been shewed, *naturally free*, and nothing being able to put him into subjection to any Earthly Power, but only by his own Consent" (Emphasis in original) (Locke 1966, 347). However, although Locke argues that all are born free and equal, he does acknowledge that equality is not the same in all circumstances.

One must ask oneself when reading Locke's idea of a state of nature: What would make man give up the freedom he has in the state of nature and voluntarily place it in the hands of another power? He addresses this issue directly:

> If Man in the State of Nature be so free, as has been said; if he be absolute Lord of his own Person and Possessions, equal to the greatest, and subject to no Body, why will he part with his Freedom? Why will he give up this Empire, and subject himself to the Dominion and Control of any other Power? . . . 'Tis obvious to Answer, that though in the state of Nature he hath such a right, yet the Enjoyment of it is very uncertain, and constantly exposed to the Invasion of others. (Locke 1966, 350)

According to Locke, the main motivating factor for individuals to enter into a social contract with a society was for the preservation of their property and safety from the invasion of others. The state of nature was very uncertain, with people's rights under constant threat, and these conditions were what drove them to enter into a social contract with others for protection. He argues that property right is something that a man brings with him when he enters into a contract with society. Society does not control or, except in certain cases, regulate it. This means that society and government exist primarily to protect this individual's property right. He makes a good point that even with all the freedom in the world, if one does not have safety, one could not freely enjoy that liberty in the state of nature.

As Grotius had also pointed out, the difficulties encountered in the state of nature are exasperated with the increase in human population, the decrease in natural resources, and the economic inequality which accompanies the introduction of the use of money. Handling these issues individually turns out to be an almost impossible feat, and men are therefore driven to seek the protection of a society and the comfort found in the commonwealth.

The great defect of the state of nature was that it lacked the organization provided by written laws or "neutral" judges. Locke claims that whatever is evil or good is automatically deemed so by natural law and positive law simply acted as the enforcer of such judgments. In this sense, Locke's state of nature sounds a bit chaotic, with no hierarchical form of authority to maintain order: "Any one in the state of nature may punish another. . . . Naturally there is no superiority or jurisdiction of one, over another" (Locke 1966, 272). In other words, everyone in the state of nature has executive power and gets the same punishment for a crime committed. Locke is prepared for the opponents that he knows he will encounter to this idea:

> I doubt not but it will be objected, that it is unreasonable for men to be judges in their own cases, that self-love will make men partial to themselves and their friends . . . that ill nature, passion and revenge will carry them too far in punishing others . . . and that therefore God hath certainly appointed Government to restrain the partiality and violence of men. (Locke 1966, 275)

He further explains that men leave the state of nature primarily to avoid a constant state of war. The state of nature is lacking several things in order to be as safe as a society, such as an established, promulgated law and a "neutral" judge with the authority to determine the differences arising from that law and bring the state of war to a finish. Here Locke makes a point similar to Vitoria and Grotius emphasizing the need for a universal, neutral court or judge and the importance of having a law promulgated openly and clearly to the public.

Locke does believe that entering into a social contract with other humans and coming together as a society is a good idea for the betterment of the human population, but it is not absolutely necessary and can only be legitimate if a man consents to it himself. Thomas Hobbes, an influential philosopher of natural rights, stated that individuals in the state of nature had the freedom to pursue their survival in the company of others or not. They did not have an obligation to respect the rights of others and that was why the state of nature was also a continuous state of war. Locke, however, sees it differently: natural law and natural rights do coexist, but natural law demands respect for the rights of others. He claims that individuals have a responsibility to respect the rights of others even in the state of nature. Similar to Vitoria and Grotius, Locke stresses the importance and necessity for a majority rule in order to avoid chaos, confusion, and dissension, and he also refers to the idea of the society as a body, needing unification in order to persevere. As we have seen, Vitoria also referred often to society and commonwealth as a body as well and used this analogy to emphasize the importance for all its members to work together to achieve the same goal: the safety and preservation of the common good.

6.3 FORMS OF GOVERNMENT

Even though Locke describes the ways in which a government can be a remedy for the chaos inherent in the state of nature, he also tells his readers that absolute monarchs are just simple, mortal men prone to error like everyone else, if not more, and reminds his readers of the dangers that come with placing all the power in the hands of just one person:

> I desire to know what kind of government that is, and how much better it is than the state of nature, where one man commanding a multitude, has the liberty to be judge in his own case, and may do to all his subjects whatever he pleases. . . . Much better is it in the state of nature wherein Men are not bound to submit to the unjust will of another. (Locke 1966, 276)

Contrary to Vitoria, who was in favor of the idea of placing the power of the commonwealth in the hands of just one person due to its unifying factor, Locke is so adamantly against absolute monarchy that he says it has no place within *any* kind of civil society. The main reason why absolute monarchy still existed in spite of its obvious flaws as a civil form of government was because of people's resistance to change. As he later asks, and with very good reason, "What Security, *what Fence* is there in such a State, *against the Violence and Oppression of this Absolute Ruler?*" (Emphasis in original) (Locke 1966, 328). Vitoria, from a totally different perspective, had argued that there was no less liberty under a monarchy than under an aristocracy or timocracy. Not only that, monarchy was actually better at preserving the peace of the commonwealth due to the unifying presence of a single ruler:

> Nobody can be unaware how much more effective monarchy is when it comes to the preservation of peace. In commonwealths where many men share government, it is inevitable that rivals for office should spend their efforts in quarrels and seditions, tearing the commonwealth apart with different policies. . . . Therefore the best form of government is monarchy, just as the universe is controlled by a single Lord and Ruler. (Locke 1966, 20)

Locke, Vitoria, and Grotius, as well as most political thinkers, agree that tyranny does not have a place in any kind of civil society. Locke warns that contrary to what one may think, tyranny is a threat neither found solely in monarchies nor necessarily concentrated in just one person:

> 'Tis a Mistake to think this Fault is proper only to Monarchies; other Forms of Government are liable to it, as well as that. For where-ever the Power that is put in any hands for the Government of the People, and the Preservation of their Properties, is applied to other ends, and made use of to impoverish, harass, or subdue them to the Arbitrary and Irregular Commands of those that have it: There it presently becomes *Tyranny*, whether those that thus use it are one or many. (Emphasis in original) (Locke 1966, 400)[2]

In order to avoid the threat of tyranny, Locke expresses the need of limits on power and divides government into three powers: the legislative, executive, and federative. Of these three, the legislative is the supreme power.

The power of the legislative, coming from the people, has strict boundaries. First, it has to follow established laws; second, those laws have to be designed for only the good of the people; and third, taxes are not to be raised on property without the consent of the people. The biggest blow to a government and a guarantee for its dissolution is when its legislative has been affected. Although the legislative was for Locke the supreme power in the government, the ultimate power never left the people, since they could still remove or replace the legislative when it was not delivering its promises of safeguarding the commonwealth. Locke's argument, echoing Vitoria's, that "the *Community* may be said in this respect to be *always the Supreme Power*" (Emphasis in original) is in direct opposition to Grotius's idea that once the power has been transferred from the people to the government, it cannot be taken back under any circumstances.

Even though Locke puts strong emphasis on the importance of the separation and balance of powers in a state, later in his treatise he displays a consistency similar to that of Vitoria by arguing, like Grotius, that in times of need, exceptions can be made to the law by the government. Locke describes this power as prerogative, which is the power the people permit their rulers to do things of their own free choice, even if it goes against written law. Of course, these exceptions could only be made with the good of the community in mind. Locke uses the example of the king calling Parliaments in England, which was the choice of only the king, but was done ultimately for the common good. It seems that giving the government and the lawmakers this kind of loophole in the law and a freedom to manipulate things can be risky, since many times they make them suit their own agendas.

Locke does address an obvious question: "*Who shall be Judge* when this Power is made a right use of?" (Emphasis in original) (Locke 1966, 379). Although one would hope that Locke would offer a logical answer to this dilemma, he does not. Locke is vague and unconvincing in his response. He says that if the power is used wrongly, there is no solid remedy and the people's only answer is to appeal to God. This is where the danger of the prerogative power granted to rulers primarily lies. Since the law is not "official," there is no one to answer to, no judge but God.

6.4 STATE OF WAR

A state of war is entered as soon as someone unjustifiably uses force. Locke argues that force and moral right are two totally different things and that the former in no way gives rise to the latter. Whoever is guilty of being the aggressor is a criminal. Also, similar to Grotius, Locke believed that once a state of war had begun, all ties of obligation and hierarchy were nullified. Even though members of the commonwealth cannot exactly punish their king for doing things with which they may not agree, if a state of war is entered between the king and his subjects, it "*levels the Parties*, cancels all former relation of Reverence, Respect, and *Superiority*" (Emphasis in original) (Locke 1966, 422). Now, who would have the authority to determine whether or not the king has acted in a way that warrants a state of war with him? Here, Locke shows some very advanced ideas for his time in the power that he gives to the people and his belief in popular sovereignty: "*The People shall be Judge*. If this be reasonable in particular Cases of private Men, why should it be otherwise in that of the greatest moment; where the Welfare of Millions is concerned, and also where the evil, if not prevented, is greater and the Redress very difficult, dear, and dangerous?" (Emphasis in original) (Locke 1966, 427).

Locke, similar to Vitoria, preaches that war should be avoided at all costs, because even in a *just* war evil is present. He describes the state of war as being different from the state of nature in that the state of war only ensues when someone violates another's rights. In Locke's theory of war, there will always be an unjust antagonist on one side and an innocent victim on the other, different from Vitoria's theory that allows the possibility for both sides to be fighting a just cause at the same time.

6.5 SLAVERY

Locke repeatedly stresses the fact that all men possess an undeniable freedom and it can only be taken away from them through death. So what about slavery? Locke describes it as "nothing else, but the *State of war continued, between a lawful Conqueror, and a Captive*" (Emphasis in original) (Locke 1966, 284). But once a contract is signed between the warring parties, this state of continuous war and slavery ceases. Locke maintains that there is only one way to lose this equality and become a "legitimate" slave, and that is during a state of war when the unjust aggressor is defeated and taken as captive rather than killed. In this case, the state of slavery becomes the continuation of the state of war, where the just victor decides to spare the captive's life and put him to work instead. This concept of slavery is an important one in Locke's work. By pointing out the limits of legitimate slavery, he ends up describing his concept of illegitimate slavery: when someone possesses absolute control over somebody else without a just cause. Locke believed that this type of slavery was what the absolute monarchs were trying to impose on their unknowing subjects. Here we see an example of something that may have been interpreted by people who were subject to any kind of oppression as more of a fight for the equality of *all* mankind than it actually was.

These new ideas challenged the principles that supported colonial slave labor during the late eighteenth and early nineteenth centuries. Although slaves already had their own traditions that supported resistance, this spread of egalitarian ideas among European intellectuals was a crucial element in developing a collective force among the disparate slave population. However, many times these ideas often caused a wrong impression of the revolutionary movements that were taking place throughout Europe (such as the French Revolution) as being more focused on the freedom and equality of all mankind than they actually were. Nonetheless, they did serve as a strong unifying force for insurgents and helped them come together under a common identity and purpose. This spread of information among rebels served as a mobilizing force for future revolutions, such as the Haitian Revolution that resulted in the Haitian Constitution of 1805.[3]

When addressing conquest, Locke makes it abundantly clear that he is not in favor of it at all. The threat of conquest can completely destroy a society and its government, dissolving entirely the necessary union and returning the people back to a state of nature. He believes that power used during conquest is a despotic power that is absolute and arbitrary and claims that the necessity to have the consent of the people before having power over them is not acknowledged "in the noise of war" during a conquest. Therefore, conquest does not count as an official way to set up a government. Locke again uses the example of pirates and robbers to prove that force does not give conquerors entitlement:

> Should a Robber break into my House, and with a Dagger at my Throat, make me seal Deeds to convey my Estate to him, would this give him any Title? Just such a Title by his Sword, has an *unjust Conqueror*, who forces me into Submission. The Injury and the Crime is equal, whether committed by the wearer of a Crown, or some petty Villain. (Emphasis in original) (Locke 1966, 385)

He feels the same about usurpers and claims that they should never be allowed to have any kind of title but that of a usurper. Even a conqueror in a just war does not have the right to take the liberty, life, or property of the conquered. As Pope Innocent IV declared in the thirteenth century (in reference to the rights of Muslims), these things cannot be taken from someone forcefully, because they belong to each individual under natural law: "Ownership, possession and jurisdiction can belong to 'infidels' licitly . . . for these things were made not only for the faithful but for every rational creature" (Innocent IV 1570). This idea was later adopted by theologians during the sixteenth century and is voiced in Vitoria's argument on the American Indians' natural right to dominion. The American Indians had their own properties and land before the arrival of the Spanish conquistadors, and under natural law, these could not be taken from them.

6.6 PROPERTY RIGHT

Locke speaks at length about property as a fundamental part of his argument on natural rights. Like Vitoria and Grotius, he argues that every man has property in the state of nature and that God has given mankind the world and all its land to put to use and appropriate it through labor. Similar to Grotius, Locke argues that labor is the way for an individual to obtain private property and put the land to use, and whatever property a man has worked on with his own hands is considered his.

Another point that Locke stresses regarding property right is that man should not abuse this power. One should never take more than is needed to survive and be able to enjoy life and take care of one's family. Although this idea once may have been plausible, "the Race of men have now spread themselves to all the corners of the World, and do infinitely exceed the small number (which) was at the beginning" (Locke 1966, 293). The world's population doubled, tripled, and even quadrupled from the "beginning" to the seventeenth and eighteenth centuries and therefore had rendered this rather simplistic view of property more Utopian than a feasible reality. In addition, the introduction of money, which caused inequality, had severely complicated things and had increased the numbers of violations of the law of nature. One can sense a certain degree of idealism when Locke speaks of the simplified and uncorrupted "beginning": "Before the desire of having more than Men needed had altered the intrinsic value of things" (Locke 1966, 294). Money had allowed men the freedom of enlarging their possessions to more than they needed. Locke concludes that the only real value of money was what was placed on it by the consent of the majority, and that this had become the way to accumulate properties beyond one's personal needs. The question is, Was he criticizing the corrupting influence of money or was this more a way of justifying a capitalist accumulation of properties beyond the question of pure necessity?

While seeming to display a yearning for the simplicity of the "beginning" times, Locke also preaches the need to be adaptable to change: "Things of this World are in so constant a Flux, that nothing remains long in the same State . . . to what gross absurdities the following of a Custom, when Reason has left it, may lead" (Locke 1966, 372). Notwithstanding, it seems clear that he does not approve of the accumulation of wealth beyond one's needs. He may acknowledge that it is absurd to try and cling to customs that have become obsolete or impractical, but at the same time he deplores this development toward capitalism. It is without a doubt that John Locke completely revolutionized Western thinking with his ideas on natural law and human rights. His philosophy on the state of nature and the social contract among communities laid the foundation for liberalism by emphasizing individual rights at the same time as stressing the need for people to respect the rights of others in order for the societal system to function well. These influential theories were ones he shared for the most part with his predecessors, Francisco de Vitoria and Hugo Grotius, who also played a vital role in transforming conventional thought on people's natural rights. In spite of their geographical and chronological separations, these three brilliant thinkers shared one consistent view: that every human being was entitled to their life, which could never be forcibly taken, and to their liberty and property, unless these were handed over voluntarily or lost in battle. These ideas have been echoed in revolutions, wars, and treatises throughout history until today.

NOTES

1. Filmer had also argued that patriarchal and political power were one and the same and that combined these resulted in despotic power. Locke emphasized that these three powers were different and separate from one another. Patriarchal power was limited in its scope; it was the power parents had over their kids until they came to the age of reason. Political power was much greater and since it obtained its authority to enforce the law of nature from the consent of individuals, it carried with it the power to do virtually anything to preserve the rights of the people for the common good. Despotic power was an absolute power that neither came from nature nor was

made by a contract. With this power a man could take away the life of another whenever he chose to.

2. The thirty tyrants ruled in Athens 404–403 B.C., the tyrants of Syracuse were advised by Plato, and the Decemviri were ten individuals who ruled the Roman Republic and were forced out of the government for tyrannical behavior in 449 B.C.

3. The Haitian Constitution stated that any black person arriving to the country would become a citizen and granted equality to all former slaves.

Conclusion

The goal of this study is to illuminate the following points: (1) the theories discussed are still relevant in present-day politics and relations between nations and states; (2) the knowledge of their evolution throughout time is crucial in their current application; (3) by reading these prominent works of the period, one can get a sense of what was important during that time in society. This is especially the case with the Spanish conquest and its repercussions, particularly the attempt to reformulate the old Roman canon of law to fit into a new, more universal context.

The relationship between colonial expansion, the law of nations, and human rights was at the center of many discussions throughout Spain and the New World by intellectuals, jurists, theologians, and other scholars, in an attempt to find a way to reconcile these often contradictory notions. This critical reconstruction of Francisco de Vitoria's philosophical and juridical work focuses on the substantial shift that he initiated in the political ideology of sixteenth-century Spain. Vitoria resorted to theology to answer questions of statehood, such as the source and objective of law and society, the basis and goal of sovereignty, the role of political authority in matters of the state, the hierarchy and foundations of order in international politics, and the place of political power in human affairs.

In studying Vitoria's ideas and how these served to introduce the theory of an international community, I have found myself confronted with several disconcerting contradictions and discrepancies, which might have led me to question the sincerity of some of the solutions he sets forth concerning the treatment of the American Indians. However, regardless of the authenticity of his "humanitarian" feeling, I still believe it is crucial to recognize the impact of Vitoria's ideas on the political, theological, philosophical, and cultural world of sixteenth-century Spain and Europe, the effects of which can still be seen today. His concept of constitutional power and moral majority has thought-provoking implications for current-day scholarship, as universal legal order is being challenged by terrorist groups: "Sovereign authority is historically constituted, but the embedded freedoms of constituent human power can emerge at any time to challenge constitutionally protected rights and borders" (Tung 2014, 23).

It is difficult to pinpoint the origin of an idea, especially one as pivotal as that of an international community, or the origin of anything in history for that matter. As Nietzsche so eloquently describes, "What is found at the historical beginning of things is not the inviolable identity of their origin; it is the dissension of other things" (Foucault 1984, 79). However, one thing that is absolutely certain is the fact that by discussing and questioning the juridical and theological bases for Spanish sovereignty in the New World, Vitoria completely revolutionized the already-existing but more limited theories of jus gentium (law of nations) and *bellum justum* (just war).

José María Beneyto's book, *At the Origins of Modernity*, is based on information gathered from an international project conducted by the Institute for European Studies of the San Pablo University in Madrid and a seminar on Vitoria and International Law that took place in July 2015. It states that there has been a renewed interest in Vitoria over the last several years due to the increased focus on global topics such as colonialism, imperialism, and the legitimation of military interventions. Vitoria was well ahead of his time and contributed more to law theory than just helping bridge the gap between the Middle Ages and Modernity, by providing a framework for addressing present-day challenges. A good example of its relevance in modern politics was given by former senator for New York and author of *On the Law of Nations*, Daniel Moynihan, when he invoked Vitorian ideology in an attempt to put limits to the systematic imperialistic violation of international law during the presidency of Ronald Reagan.

Vitoria's most valuable contribution to the modern just war theory and international law in general was his idea that the world would be a more peaceful place if nations came together to form an international community, which would develop from the common humanity and nature inherent in all men. He stated that the law of nations' main objective ought to be to help solve conflicts between cultures and create an open dialogue among all nations, so that all voices could be heard. Vitoria's idea of a worldwide system of law that could be used in relations between nations was based on the irrefutable authority of natural law, which would in turn create a common agenda for all to adhere to and transfer the focus of authority from divine law and the pope to natural law and a secular sovereign.

This reformulation of political ideas during the sixteenth century in Spain was also used in subsequent centuries, particularly by Hugo Grotius and John

Locke, and in the establishment of the League of Nations and later, the UN. Many of Vitoria's ideas can also be found in the Declaration of Independence and the American Constitution. Perhaps the best-known document articulating this notion of individual human rights voiced by Vitoria, Locke, and Grotius is the United States' Declaration of Independence, which justifies the independence of the United States from UK by asserting inalienable natural rights, including a right of revolution. Although this pronouncement was originally made with the purpose of justifying the American colonies' revolution from their "mother country" during the American Revolution, the Declaration of Independence has been defined as a model by which the Constitution of the United States should be interpreted. The second sentence of the Declaration, perhaps the most legendary, is the one that most closely echoes the ideas of Vitoria, Grotius, and Locke: "We hold these truths to be self-evident, that *all men are created equal*, that they are endowed by their Creator with certain *unalienable Rights*, that among these are *Life, Liberty and the pursuit of Happiness*" (Emphasis in original). These three commanding scholars' ethical perspectives of political society were strongly influential in the development of a modern conception of politics today.

The presence of the fundamental principles of the theory of international law that have remained intact throughout its evolution raises other important questions. Have we not been able to learn from history's lessons and are we still making the same mistakes, with the same mentality that existed in the philosophical and political processes of antiquity and the sixteenth century? Has any further development of this theory been halted? Or are these fundamental principles so vital to the whole theory of law that they can never be replaced? Maybe we will never know the answers to these and other pertinent questions, since we cannot determine the result of a movement that is still in progress.

It is also extremely difficult to determine the authoritative origins of such a vast intellectual movement, since the cultures and societies in this world merge and exchange ideas and beliefs continuously. Foucault addresses a similar issue: "It is wrong to search for descent in an uninterrupted continuity" (Foucault 1984, 83). Attempting to grasp the "truth" as it was presented during sixteenth-century Spain and in today's day and age is an illusory objective, because "truth is undoubtedly the sort of error that cannot be refuted because it was hardened into an unalterable form in the long-baking process of history" (Foucault 1984, 79). Seen from this perspective, true facts can no longer be separated from false ones because they have been entrenched in the historical process together for so long that they have lost distinction from each other. Anthony Pagden warns against analyzing or comparing earlier theories on international law with current-day situations: "By describing the battles of the early modern world in modern terms, by making Francisco de

Vitoria the remote ancestor of the Charter of the United Nations or the Bill of Rights, the specificity of the conflict is lost, and with it the possibility of its significance as a process over time" (Pagden 1994, x).

However, despite all the obstacles and inconsistencies that I found during the research process, it is still very important to recognize the impact of Vitorian ideology on law and political theory. The flexibility of Vitoria's concept of power offers compelling incentives for contemporary scholarship, and I am more convinced than ever that in order to understand the true nature of contemporary international law, as well as the political ideology of a time and its influence on the development of international politics, it is crucial to analyze Vitoria's theories in their sociohistorical context. Thus, one can come to a better understanding of today's political legitimizing process of invasions of or actions against other countries.

Appendix A
Further Reading

Antoninus, Marcus Aurelius. 1989. *The Meditations of Marcus Aurelius Antoninus.* Translated by A.S.L. Farquharson and selected by R.B. Rutherford. Oxford: Oxford University Press.

Araujo, Orestes. 1948. *Las doctrinas internacionalistas de Fray Francisco de Vitoria.* Montevideo: LJGU.

Barcia Trelles, Camilo. 1928. *Francisco de Vitoria, fundador del Derecho Internacional moderno.* Valladolid: Universidad de Valladolid.

Bardo, Fassbender and Anne Peters, editors. 2012. *The Oxford Handbook of the History of International Law.* Oxford: Oxford University Press.

Beltrán de Heredia, Vicente. 1939. *Francisco de Vitoria.* Barcelona: Editorial Labor.

———. 1928. *Los manuscritos de Fray Francisco de Vitoria, O.P.: estudio critico de introducción a sus lecturas y relecciones.* Madrid: Santo Domingo el Real.

———. 1972. *Miscelánea Beltrán de Heredia: Colección de artículos sobre historia de la teología española.* Guadalajara: Editorial OPE.

Blackburn, Robin. 1997. *The Making of New World Slavery: From the Baroque to the Modern*, 1492–1800. London: Verso.

Botero, Giovanni. 1956. *The Reason of State.* Introduction by D.P. Waley. New Haven, CT: Yale University Press.

Brett, Stephen F. 1994. *Slavery and the Catholic Tradition.* New York: Peter Lang.

Burkhart, Louise M. 1989. *The Slippery Earth: Nahua-Christian Moral Dialogue in Sixteenth-Century Mexico.* Tucson: University of Arizona Press.

Bull, Hedley. 1977. *The Anarchical Society: A Study of Order in World Politics.* New York City: Macmillan.

———. 1968. "The Grotian Conception of International Society." In *Diplomatic Investigations*, 51–73. Cambridge: Cambridge University Press.

Bull, Hedley and Benedict Kingsbury, editors. 1990. *Hugo Grotius and International Relations.* Oxford: Clarendon Press.

Butler, William E. and James Brown Scott. 2008. *Catholic Conception of International Law: Francisco De Vitoria, Founder of the Modern Law of Nations. Francisco*

Suarez, Founder of the Modern Philosophy of Law in General and in Particular of the Law of Nations; a Critical Examination and a Justified Appreciation. Clark, NJ: The Lawbook Exchange Ltd.

Cañizares-Esguerra, Jorge. 2001. *How to Write the History of the New World: Histories, Epistemologies, and Identities in the Eighteenth-Century Atlantic World.* Stanford: Stanford University Press.

Capizzi, Joseph. 2002. "The Children of God: Natural Slavery in the Thought of Aquinas and Vitoria." In *Theological Studies*, 31–52. Oxford: Oxford University Press.

Castilla Urbano, Francisco. 1990. *Filosofía política e indio americano: el pensamiento de Francisco de Vitoria.* Madrid: Universidad Complutense de Madrid.

Clendinnen, Inga. 1987. *Ambivalent Conquests: Maya and Spaniard in Yucatan, 1517-1570.* Cambridge: Cambridge University Press.

———. 1981. *Aztecs: An Interpretation.* Cambridge: Cambridge University Press.

Columbus, Christopher. 1969. *The Four Voyages of Christopher Columbus; Being His Own Log-Book, Letters and Dispatches with Connecting Narrative Drawn from the Life of the Admiral by his son Hernando Colón and Other Contemporary Historians.* Edited by J.M. Cohen. Harmondsworth: Penguin.

Cortés, Hernán. 1993. *Cartas de relación.* Edited by Angel Delgado Gómez. Madrid: Castalia.

———. 1971. *Letters from Mexico.* Edited by Anthony R. Pagden and introduction by J.H. Elliott. New York: Grossman Publishers.

Cruz Cruz, Juan. 2008. "La soportable fragilidad de la ley natural: consignación del *ius gentium* en Vitoria." In *Ley y dominio en Francisco de Vitoria*, 13–40. Pamplona: Ediciones Universidad de Navarra.

Davidson, J.S. 1994. "The Rights of Indigenous Peoples in Early International Law." *Canterbury Law Review, vol. 5*: 391–423.

Díaz del Castillo, Bernal. 1989. *Historia verdadera de la conquista de la Nueva España.* Edited by Carmelo Sáenz de Santamaría. Madrid: Alianza.

Diego Carro, Venancio. 1951. *La teología y los teólogos-juristas españoles ante la conquista de America.* Salamanca: (s.n.).

———. 1944. "Las controversias de Indias u las ideas teológico-medievales que las preparan y explican." *Ciencia tomista* 209: 5–32.

Edwards, Charles. 1981. *Hugo Grotius, The Miracle of Holland: A Study in Political and Legal Thought.* Chicago: Chicago University Press.

Elliot, John Huxtable. 1964. *Imperial Spain, 1469-1716.* New York: St. Martin's Press.

———. 1963. *The Revolt of the Catalans, a Study in the Decline of Spain, 1598-1640.* Cambridge: Cambridge University Press.

Fernandez Santa María, J.A. 1977. *The State, War, and Peace: Spanish Political Thought in the Renaissance, 1516-1599.* Cambridge: Cambridge University Press.

Flores Galindo, Alberto. 1988. *Buscando un inca.* Lima: Editorial Horizonte.

Forde, Steven. 2001. "Natural Law, Theology, and Morality in Locke." *American Journal of Science, vol. 45*: 396–409.

Foster, George M. 1960. *Culture and Conquest: America's Spanish Heritage.* Chicago: Quadrangle Books.
Fraile, Guillermo. 1971. *Historia de la filosofía española.* Madrid: Editorial Católica.
Freyre, Gilberto. 1956. *The Masters and the Slaves (Casa-grade & senzala). A Study in the Development of Brazilian Civilization.* New York City: Knopf.
Gandía, Enrique de. 1952. *Francisco de Vitoria y el Nuevo Mundo: El problema teológico y jurídico del hombre americano y la independencia de América.* Buenos Aires: Editorial Vasca Ekin.
García y García, A. 1997. "The Spanish School of the Sixteenth and Seventeenth Centuries: A Precursor of the Theory of Human Rights." *Ratio Juris.* Oxford: Hart Publishing: 25–35.
García Villoslada, R. 1938. "La Universidad de París durante los estudios de Francisco de Vitoria." *Analecta Gregoriana, vol. 9*: 384–401.
González Echevarría, Roberto. 1990. *Myth and Archive: A Theory of Latin American Narrative.* Cambridge: Cambridge University Press.
Gorosquieta Reyes, Javier. "El sistema de las ideas tributaries en los teólogos y moralistas principals de la escuela de Salamanca (siglox XVI y XVII)." PhD diss., Universidad Complutense, 1972.
Grant, Ruth. 1987. *John Locke's Liberalism.* Chicago: University of Chicago Press.
Gregg, Samuel. 2020. "Natural Law and the Law of Nations." *Acton Institute.* http://www.nlnrac.org/earlymodern/law-of-nations.
Gruzinski, Serge. 1989. *Man-Gods in the Mexican Highlands: Indian Power and Colonial Society, 15290-1800.* Translated by Eileen Corrigan. Stanford: Stanford University Press.
Hamilton, Bernice. 1963. *Political Thought in Sixteenth-Century Spain.* Oxford: Clarendon Press.
Harries, Jill. 1999. *Law and Empire in the Late Antiquity.* Cambridge; New York: Cambridge University Press.
Hartigan, Richard S. 1973. "Francesco De Vitoria and Civilian Immunity." *Political Theory* 1: 79–91.
Hooker, Richard. 1989. *Of The Laws Of Ecclesiastical Polity.* Cambridge University Press.
Huntington, Samuel. 2011. *The Clash of Civilizations and the Remaking of World Order.* New York: Simon & Schuster.
Keene, Edward. 2002. *Beyond the Anarchical Society: Grotius, Colonialism and Order in World Politics.* Cambridge: Cambridge University Press.
Kingsbury, Ben. 1996. "Grotius, Law, and Moral Skepticism: Theory and Practice in the Thought of Hedley Bull." In *Classical Theories of International Relations,* edited by Clark and Newmann. New York: Macmillan: 42–70.
Knight, W.S.M. 1925. *The Life and Works of Hugo Grotius.* London: Sweet and Maxwell.
Koskenniemi, Martti. 2002. "Empire and International Law: The Real Spanish Contribution." In *Global Community, and Political Justice Since Vitoria.* Farnham: 108–112.

Kupperman, Karen Ordahl, ed. 1995. *America in European Consciousness, 1493-1750.* Chapel Hill: University of North Carolina Press, 1995.

Larson, Brooke. 1992. *Colonialismo y transformación agrarian en Bolivia: Cochabamba 1550-1990.* La Paz: Ceres/Hisbol.

León Montilla, Miguel, ed. 1962. *The Broken Spears: The Aztec Account of the Conquest of Mexico.* Translation by Lysander Kemp. Boston: Beacon Press.

Leyes de Burgos de 1512 y Leyes de Valladolid de 1513: Reproducción facsimilar de los manuscritos que se conservan en el archivo general de Indias (Sevilla) en las secciones de indiferente general Leg. 419, Lib. IV y patronato, legajo 174 ramo 1, respectivamente. 1991. Historical analysis and transcription by M. Luisa Martinez de Salinas. Institutional Juridical studies by Rogelio Perez Bustamante. Presentation by Antonio Pedrol. Burgos: Fundación para el desarrollo provincial.

Lissarrague, S. 1947. *La teoría del poder en Francisco de Vitoria.* Madrid: Instituto de Estudios Políticos.

Losada, Ángel. 1963. *Tratados políticos de Juan Ginés de Sepúlveda.* Madrid: Instituto de Estudios Políticos.

Lucombe, D.E. 1982. "The State of Nature and the Origin of State." In *The Cambridge History of Later Medieval Philosophy: From the Rediscovery of Aristotle to the Disintegration of Scholasticism 1100-1600.* Cambridge: Cambridge University Press.

Lupher, David A. 2003. *Romans in a New World: Classical Models in Sixteenth-Century Spanish America.* Michigan: University of Michigan Press.

Mantilla, Yuri. 2012. *Francisco de Vitoria and the Spanish Scholastic Perspective on Law and the Conquest of the Incan Empire.* Aberdeen: Aberdeen University.

Maritain, Jacques. 1994. *The Person and the Common Good.* University of Notre Dame Press.

Martínez Alier, Verena. 1974. *Marriage, Class and Colour in Nineteenth-Century Cuba: A Study in Racial Attitudes and Sexual Values in a Slave Society.* Cambridge: Cambridge University Press.

Mathisen, Ralph W, ed. 2001. *Law, Society, and Authority in Late Antiquity.* New York: Oxford University Press.

Menéndez Pidal, Ramón. 1963. *El padre Las Casas: su doble personalidad.* Madrid: Espasa-Calpe.

Menéndez-Reigada, Ignacio. 1929. *El sistema ético-jurídico de Vitoria sobre el Derecho de gentes: conferencia inugural de la Cátedra Francisco de Vitoria en la Universidad de Salamanca (curso 1928 a 1929).* Salamanca: Establecimiento Tipográfico de Calatrava.

Meron, Theodore. 1991. "Common Rights of Mankind in Gentili, Grotius and Suarez." *American Journal of International* Law: 85–111.

Miller, Fred D. and Carrie-Ann Biondi, ed. 2015. "A History of the Philosophy of Law from the Ancient Greeks to the Scholastics." In *A Treatise of Legal Philosophy and General Jurisprudence*, vol. 6. New York: Springer Dordrecht Heidelberg.

Mirete, J.L. 2001. "Maquiavelo y la recepción de su teoría del Estado en España (siglos XVI y XVII)." *Anales de Derecho* 19: 139–146.

Morris, John F. 2000. "The Contribution of Francisco De Vitoria to the Scholastic Understanding of the Principle of the Common Good." *Modern Schoolman* 78, no. 1: 9–33.

Moser, Paul K., and Arnold Vander Nat, eds. 1987. *Human Knowledge: Classical and Contemporary Approaches*. New York: Oxford University Press.

Motolinía, Toribio de. 1988. *Historia de los indios de la Nueva España*. Introduction and notes by Giuseppe Bellini. Madrid: Alianza.

Nellen, Henk J.M., ed. 2014. *Hugo Grotius: A Lifelong Struggle for Peace in Church and State, 1583-1645*. Leiden: Brill Academic Publishers.

Nichols, Barry. 1962. *An Introduction to Roman Law*. Oxford: Oxford University Press.

Neff, Stephen. 2014. *Justice Among Nations: A History of International Law*. Cambridge, MA: Harvard University Press.

Neville Figgis, John. 1916. *Studies of Political Thought from Gerson to Grotius, 1414-1625*. Cambridge: Cambridge University Press.

Nys, Ernest. 1882. "Le Droit de guerre et les précurseurs de Grotius." *Revue de Droit International et de Législation compare, vol. 22*: 371–384.

Palacios Rubios, Juan López and Matías de Paz. 1954. *De las Islas del Mar Océano y Del dominio de los Reyes de España sobre los indios*. Mexico: Fondo de Cultura Económica.

Parker, Geoffrey. 1988. *The Grand Strategy of Philip II*. New Haven: Yale University Press.

Pastor Bodmer, Beatriz. 1992. *The Armature of Conquest: Spanish Accounts of the Discovery of America, 1492-1589*. Stanford: Stanford University Press.

Polls, Adamantia and Peter Schwab. 1979. *Human Rights: Cultural and Ideological Perspectives*. Westport, CT: Praeger.

Prescott, William H. 1936. *History of the Conquest of Mexico, and History of the Conquest of Peru*. New York: Modern Library.

———. 1884. *History of the Reign of Ferdinand and Isabella*. New York: John B. Alden.

Quevedo y Villegas, Francisco de. 1946. *Política de Dios y Gobierno de Cristo*. Buenos Aires: Espasa-Calpe.

———. 1950. *Vida de Marco Bruto*. Buenos Aires: Espasa-Calpe.

Ramos Pérez, Demetrio. 1984. *La ética de la conquista de América: Francisco de Vitoria y la Escuela de Salamanca*. Madrid: Consejo Superior de Investigaciones Científicas.

Renteln, Alison. 2013. *International Human Rights: Universalism versus Relativism*. New Orleans: Quid Pro.

Ribeiro, Darcy. 1969. *Las Américas y la civilización. Tomo 1: La civilización occidental y nosotros: Los pueblos testimonio*. Translated by Renzo Pi Hugarte. Buenos Aires: Centro Editor de América Latina.

Ricard, Robert. 1966. *The Spiritual Conquest of Mexico; an Essay on the Apostolate and the Evangelizing Methods of the Mendicant Orders in New Spain, 1523-1572*. Translated by Lesley Byrd Simpson. Berkeley: University of California Press.

Rodríguez, Jaime E. 1998. *The Independence of Spanish America*. Cambridge: Cambridge University Press.

Rommen, Heinrich Albert. 1998. *The Natural Law: A Study in Legal and Social History and Philosophy*. Translated by Thomas Hanley. Carmel: Liberty Fund.

Rozat Dupeyron, Guy. 1993. *Indios imaginarios e indios reales en los relatos de la conquista de México*. Mexico: Tava Editorial.

Sahagún, Bernardino de (Father). 1990. *Historia general de las cosas de Nueva España*. Edited by Juan Carlos Temprano. Madrid: Historia 16.

Salamanca, Beatriz. 2015. "Early Modern Controversies of Mobility within the Spanish Empire: Francisco de Vitoria and the Peaceful Right to Travel." *Tropos* 3: 14–21.

Sanchez, Luis. 1959. *El concepto del Estado en el pensamiento español del siglo XVI*. Madrid: Instituto de Estudios Políticos.

Schroder, Peter. 2010. "Vitoria, Gentili, Bodin: Sovereignty and the Law of Nations." In *The Roman Foundations of the Law of Nations: Alberto Gentili and the Justice of Empire*. Oxford University Press.

Schwartz, Stuart B. 1985. *Sugar Plantations in the Formation of Brazilian Society: Bahia, 1550-1835*. Cambridge: Cambridge University Press.

Seminario americanista. 1976. *Juan Ginés de Sepúlveda y su crónica indiana: en el IV centenario de su muerte, 1573-1973*. Valladolid and Pozoblanco: Universidad de Valladolid and Ayuntamiento.

Smith-Darian, Eve and Peter Fitzpatrick, editors. 1999. *Laws of the Postcolonial*. Ann-Arbor: University of Michigan Press.

Stern, Steve J. 1982. *Peru's Indian Peoples and the Challenge of Spanish Conquest: Huamanga to 1640*. Madison: University of Wisconsin Press.

Steuco, Agostino. 2007. *De perenni philosophia libri X*. Stuttgart: Frommann-Holzboog.

Strauss, Leo. 1953. *Natural Right and History*. Chicago: University of Chicago Press.

Swanson, Scott G. 1997. "The Medieval Foundations of John Locke's Theory of Natural Rights: Rights of Subsistence and the Principle of Extreme Necessity." *Historical or History of Political Thought* 18: 399–459.

Truyol y Serra, Antonio. 1946. *Los principios del derecho público en Francisco de Vitoria*. Madrid: Ediciones cultura hispánica.

Valdés, Alfonso de. 1952. *Alfonso de Valdés and the Sack of Rome: Dialogue of Lactancio and an Archdeacon*. Translated by John E. Longhurst. New Mexico: University of New Mexico Press.

Valdés, Alfonso de and Juan de Valdés. 1850. *Dos diálogos*. Edited by Luis Usoz y Río. Madrid.

Valdés, Juan de. 1965. *Diálogo de Mercurio y Carón*. Edition, introduction and notes by José F. Montesinos. Madrid: Espasa-Calpe.

Vega, Garcilaso de la. 1966. *Royal Commentaries of the Incas, and General History of Peru*. Translated with an introduction by Harold V. Livermore. Foreword by Arnold J. Toynbee. Austin: University of Texas Press.

Verlag, Franz Steiner. 1979. "Michael Villey on Modern Natural Law." *Archives for Philosophy of Law and Social Philosophy* 65, no. 3: 413–430.

Viqueira Albán, Juan. 1999. *Propriety and Permissiveness in Bourbon Mexico*. Translated by Sonya Lipsett-Rivera and Sergio Rivera Ayala. Wilmington, DE: Scholarly Resources.

Von Pufendorf, Samuel. 1998. *De jure naturae et gentium*. Edited by Frank Böhlig. Berlin: Akademie Verlag.

Waldron, Jeremy. 2002. *God, Locke, and Equality: Christian Foundations in Locke's Political Thought*. Cambridge University Press.

Westbury-Jones, John. 1971. *Roman and Christian Imperialism*. New York: Kennikat Press.

Wilson, Charles. 1984. *Hugo Grotius and His World (1583-1645)*. Amsterdam: Holland University Press.

Wood, Ellen Meiksins. 2003. *Empire of Capital*. New York: Verso.

Zuckert, Michael P. 1994. *Natural Rights and the New Republicanism*. Princeton: Princeton University Press.

Bibliography

Andújar, Eduardo. 1997. "Bartolomé de Las Casas and Juan Ginés de Sepúlveda: Moral Theology versus Political Philosophy." In *Hispanic Philosophy in the Age of Discovery*, edited by Kevin White. Washington, DC: Catholic University of America.

Anghie, Anthony. 1999. "Francisco de Vitoria and the Colonial Origins of International Law." In *Laws of the Postcolonial*, edited by Eve Darain-Smith and Peter Fitzpatrick, 81–104. Ann Arbor, MI: University of Michigan Press.

——— 2001. *Imperialism, Sovereignty and the Making of International Law.* Cambridge: Cambridge University Press.

Aquinas, Thomas (Saint). 1988. *On Law, Morality, and Politics.* Edited by William P. Baumgarth and Richard J. Regan. Cambridge, UK: Hackett Publishers.

Aristotle. *Nichomean Ethics.* 1999. Introduction and translation by Terence Irwin. Indianapolis: Publishing Co.

———. 1961. *Politics and Poetics.* Introduction and translation by Lincoln Diamant. New York: Viking Press.

Baron de Montesquieu, Charles Louis de Secondat. 1777. *Complete Works of Montesquieu,* 4 vols. London. https://oll.libertyfund.org/titles/montesquieu-complete-works-vol-1-the-spirit-of-laws

Bataillon, Marcel. 1997. *Erasmo y España.* Mexico: Fondo de Cultura Económica.

Beneyto, José María. 2010. *At the Origins of Modernity: Francisco de Vitoria and the Discovery of International Law (Studies in the History of Law and Justice Book 10).* New York City: Springer.

Brett, Annabel. 2011. *Changes of State: Nature and the Limits of the City in Early Modern Natural Law.* 2011. Princeton, NJ: Princeton University Press.

———. 2012. "Francisco de Vitoria (1483-1546) and Francisco Suárez (1548-1617)." In *The Oxford Handbook of the History of International Law,* edited by Bardo Fassbender and Anne Peters. Oxford: Oxford University Press.

———. 1997. *Liberty, Right, and Nature: Individual Rights in Latter Scholastic Thought.* Cambridge: Cambridge University Press.

Butler, William E. and James Brown Scott. 2008. *Catholic Conception of International Law: Francisco De Vitoria, Founder of the Modern Law of Nations. Francisco Suaŕez, founder of the modern philosophy of law in general and in particular of the law of nations; a critical examination and a justified appreciation.* Clark, NJ: The Lawbook Exchange Ltd.

Casas, Bartolomé de las (Father) and Juan Ginés de Sepúlveda (Father). 1962. *Tratado de Indias y el doctor Sepúlveda.* Edited by Manuel Jiménez Fernández. Caracas: Academia Nacional de Historia.

Casas, Bartolomé de las (Father). 1992. *Apologética historia sumaria.* Edited by Vidal Abril Castelló. Madrid: Alianza.

———. 1982. *Brevísima relación de la destrucción de las Indias.* Edited by André Saint-Lu, Madrid: Cátedra.

———. 1951. *Historia de las Indias.* Edited by Agustín Millares Carlo and study done by Lewis Hanke. Mexico: Fondo de Cultura Económica.

———. 1974. *In defense of the Indians: The defense of the Most Reverend Lord, Don Fray Bartolomé de las Casas, of the Order of Preachers, Late Bishop of Chiapa, Against the Prosecutors and Slanderers of the People of the New World Discovered Across the Seas.* Translated, edited and annotated by Stafford Poole. Dekalb, IL: Northern Illinois University Press.

———. 1991. *The Devastation of the Indies: a Brief Account.* Translated by Herma Briffault and introduction by Bill M. Donovan. Baltimore, MD: Johns Hopkins University Press.

———. 1997. *Tratados.* Introduction by Lewis Hanke and Manuel Jiménez González. Mexico: Fondo de Cultura Económica.

Cicero. 2000. *On the Republic (De Republica), On the Laws (De Legibus).* Translated by C.W. Keyes. London: St. Edmundsbury Press Ltd.

Filmer, Robert (Sir). 2000. *Patriarcha and Other Writings.* Edited by Johann P. Sommerville, Cambridge University Press.

Foucault, Michel. 1984. "Nietzsche, Genealogy, History." In *The Foucault Reader,* edited by Paul Rabinow. New York: Pantheon Books.

Freud, Sigmund. 1961. *Civilization and Its Discontents.* London: W.W. Norton and Company.

Gaius. 1904. *Gai Institutiones or Institutes of Roman Law by Gaius.* Translation and introduction by Edward Poste. Cambridge, UK: Clarendon Press.

Getino, Luis G. Alonso. 1930. *El maestro fray Francisco de Vitoria: su vida, su doctrina y su influencia.* Madrid: Publicaciones de la asociación Francisco de Vitoria.

———.1936. *Relectiones Theologicae,* 3 vols. Edited and translated into Spanish by Luis G. Alonso. Madrid: Publicaciones de la asociación Francisco de Vitoria.

Grotius, Hugo de. 2009. *Mare Liberum, 1609-2009.* Edited and annotated by Robert Feenstra, with a general introduction by Jeroen Vervliet. Boston, MA: Brill.

———. 1949. *The Law of War and Peace (De Jure Belli ac Pacis).* New York: Walter J. Black.

Hanke, Lewis. 1974. *All Mankind Is One: A Study of the Disputation Between Bartolomé de las Casas and Juan Ginés de Sepúlveda in 1550 on the Intellectual and Religious Capacity of the American Indians.* De Kalb, IL: Northern Illinois University Press.

———. 1970. *Aristotle and the American Indians.* Bloomington: Indiana University Press.

———. 1949. *The Spanish Struggle for Justice in the Conquest of America.* Philadelphia, PA: University of Pennsylvania Press.

Hippo, Augustine of (Saint). 2000. *The City of God.* Introduction by Thomas Merton. New York: Modern Library.

Hobbes, Thomas. 1985. *Leviathan.* Edited by Macpherson, C. London: Penguin Classics.

Holmes, Arthur F. 2005. *War and Christian Ethics: Classic and Contemporary Readings on the Morality of War.* Grand Rapids, MI: Baker Academic.

"Human rights: comments and interpretations." 1948. A symposium edited by UNESCO, introduction by Jacques Maritain. https://unesdoc.unesco.org/ark:/48223/pf0000155042

Holt, James Clark. 2015. *Magna Carta,* 3rd edition. Cambridge: Cambridge University Press.

Huxley, Aldous. 1945. *Perennial Philosophy.* New York: Harper & Brothers.

Innocent IV. 1570. *Commentaria Innocentii Quarti Pont. Maximi Super Libros Quinque Decretalium.* Frankfurt.

Isidore of Seville. 1911. *Etymologiae.* Translated by W.M. Lindsay. Oxford: Oxford University Press.

Justinian. 1987. *Institutes.* Translated and introduction by Peter Birks and Grant McLeod, New York: Cornell University Press.

Kant, Immanuel. 1903. *Perpetual Peace: A Philosophical Essay.* Translated by M. Campbell Smith. London: Swan Sonnenschein.

Killoran, John B. 1987. "Aquinas and Vitoria: Two Perspectives on Slavery." In *The Medieval Tradition of Natural Law,* edited by Harold J. Johnson. Kalamazoo, MI: Medieval Institute Publications.

Locke, John. 1966. *The Second Treatise of Government (An Essay Concerning the True Original Extent and End of Civil Government), and A Letter Concerning Toleration.* Edited, with a revised introduction by J.W. Gough. Oxford: Blackwell.

Lombard, Peter. 2004. "Sentences." In *Great Medieval Thinkers: Peter Lombard.* Translation, introduction and notes by Philipp Rosemann. New York: Oxford University Press.

Machiavelli, Niccolò. 1990. *The Art of War.* Introduction by Neal Wood. New York: Da Capo Press.

———. 2003. *The Prince and Other Writings.* Translation, introduction and commentary by Wayne A. Reborn. New York: Barnes and Noble.

McKenna, Charles H., James Brown Scott and Herbert Wright. 1932. *Francisco de Vitoria Addresses in Commemoration of the Fourth Centenary of his Lectures "De Indis" and De Jure Belli" 1532-1932.* (Delivered at the Catholic University of America, May 1, 1932). Washington, DC.

Molina, Luis de (Father). 1951. *Extracts on Politics and Government.* Edited by George Albert Moore. Chevy Chase, MD: Country Dollar Press.

Monahan, Arthur P. 1994. *From Personal Duties Towards Personal Rights: Late Medieval and Early Modern Political Thought, 1300-1600.* London: McGill-Queen's University Press.

Moynihan, Daniel Patrick. 1992. *On the Law of Nations.* Cambridge, MA: Harvard University Press.

Nietzsche, Friedrich. 2005. *The Anti-Christ, Ecce-Homo, Twilight of the Idols, and Other Writings.* Edited by Aaron Ridley and Judith Norman and translated by Judith Norman. New York: Cambridge UP.

Pagden, Anthony. 1990. *Spanish Imperialism and the Political Imagination: Studies in European and Spanish-American Social and Political Theory, 1513-1830.* 1990. New Haven, CT: Yale University.

———. 2015. *The Burden of Empires: 1539 to the Present.* 2015. Cambridge: Cambridge University Press.

———. 1987. *The Languages of Political Theory in Early-Modern Europe.* 1987. Cambridge: Cambridge University Press

———. 1986. *The Fall of Natural Man: The American Indian and the Origins of Comparative Ethnology.* Cambridge: Cambridge University Press.

———. 1994. *The Uncertainties of Empire. Essays in Iberian and Ibero-American Intellectual History.* Brookfield, VT: Ashgate Publishing.

Pereña, Luciano and Carlos Baciero, eds. 1988. *Carta magna de los indios: fuentes constitucionales, 1534-1609.* Madrid: Consejo Superior de Investigaciones Científicas.

———. 1954. *La Universidad de Salamanca, forja de pensamiento político español en el siglo XVI.* Salamanca: Universidad de Salamanca.

Rotterdam, Desiderius Erasmus of. 2004. *The Complaint of Peace.* New York: Cosimo Inc.

———. 1997. *The Education of a Christian Prince.* Edited by Lisa Jardine. Cambridge: Cambridge University Press.

Sanchez Sorondo, Marcelo. 1997. "Vitoria: The Original Philosopher of Rights." *Hispanic Philosophy in the Age of Discovery: Studies in Philosophy and the History of Philosophy*, edited by Kevin White, vol. 29, 59–68. Washington, DC: Catholic University of America Press.

Scott, James Brown. 2000. *The Spanish Origin of International Law: Francisco de Vitoria and His Law of Nations.* Clark, NJ: The Lawbook Exchange.

Sepúlveda, Juan Ginés de (Father). 1979. *Tratado sobre las justas causas de la guerra contra los indios.* Study by Manuel García-Pelayo. Mexico: Fondo de Cultura Economica.

Skinner, Quentin. 2009. "A Genealogy of the Modern State." 2009. *Proceedings of the British Academy* 162: 325–370.

———. 1978. *The Foundations of Modern Political Thought*, vol. 1. Cambridge: Cambridge University Press.

Soto, Domingo de. 1964. *Relección de dominio.* Edited by J. Brufau Pratts. Granada: University of Granada.

Suárez, Francisco (Father). 1970. *Defensa de la fe católica y apostólica contra los errores del Anglicanismo: Diferencia entre la secta anglicana y la doctrina católica; Errores peculiares que el rey de Inglaterra profesa en materia de fe católica*, 3 vols. Edited by José Ramón Eguillor Muniozguren. Madrid: Instituto de Estudios Políticos, Sección Teólogos Juristas.

———. 1956. *Guerra, intervención, paz internacional.* Translation, study and notes by L. Pereña Vicente. Buenos Aires: Espasa-Calpe.

———. 1995. *On Beings of Reason.* Translation, introduction and notes by John P. Doyle. Milwaukee, WI: Marquette University Press.

———. 1964. *On Formal and Universal Unity.* Translation, introduction by J.F. Ross. Milwaukee, WI: Marquette University Press.

Subirats, Eduardo. 1994. *El continente vacio.* Mexico: Siglo XXI Editores.

———. 2003. *Memoria y exilio.* Buenos Aires: Editorial Losada.

Tierney, Brian. 2006. "Dominion of Self and Natural Rights Before Locke and After." *Transformations in Medieval and Early-Modern Rights Discourse* 59: 173–203.

———. 2001. "Permissive Natural Law and Property: Gratian to Kant." *History of Ideas* 62(3): 381–399.

———. 2004. "The Idea of Natural Rights-Origins and Persistence." *Northwestern Journal of International Human Rights.* Atlanta: Scholars.

———. 1997. *The Idea of Natural Rights: Studies on Natural Rights, Natural Law and Church Law 1150-1625.* 1997. Grand Rapids, MI: William Eerdmans-Lightning Source.

———. 2007. "Vitoria and Suarez on ius gentium, natural law, and custom." In *The Nature of Customary Law: Legal, Historical and Philosophical Perspectives*, 101–124. Cambridge: Cambridge University Press.

Tuck, Richard. 1981. *Natural Right Theories: Their Origin and Development.* New York: Cambridge UP.

———. *The Rights of War and Peace: Political Thought and the International Order from Grotius to Kant.* 2001. Oxford: Oxford University Press.

Tung, Toy-Fung. 2014. "Supernatural and Natural Sovereignty in Francisco de Vitoria: Adam and Eve's Marriage, Power, Obligatio, and Commonwealth Order." *Journal of the History of Ideas* 75(1): 45–68.

———. 2011. "Just War Claims: Historical Theory, Abu Ghraib, and Modern Rhetoric." In *International Criminal Justice: Legal and Theoretical Perspectives*, edited by George Andreopoulos.

United Nations. *Charter of Nations.* http://www.un.org/en/documents/charter.

Valenzuela-Vermehren, Luis. 2013. "The Origin and Nature of the State in Francisco de Vitoria's Moral Philosophy. *Ideas y Valores* (62): 81–103.

Vives, Juan Luis. 1940. *Concordia y discordia.* Translation and introduction by Laureano Sánchez Gallego. Mexico: Séneca.

———. 1945. *Diálogos.* 1945. Buenos Aires: Espasa-Calpe.

Vitoria, Francisco de (Father). 1995. *De Indis et iure belli relectiones Being Part of Relectiones XII.* Edited by Ernest Nys, and translated by John P. Bate. Buffalo, NY: Hein.

———. 1992. *Derechos y deberes entre indios y españoles en el nuevo mundo según Francisco de Vitoria.* Text reconstructed by Luciano Pereña Vicente. Salamanca: Cátedra/V Centenario

———. 1991. *Political Writings*. Edited by Anthony Pagden and Jeremy Lawrance. New York: Cambridge University Press.

———. 1997. *Reflection on Homicide & Commentary on Summa Theologiae IIa-IIae Q.64 (Thomas Aquinas)*. Translation, introduction and notes by John P. Doyle. Milwaukee, WI: Marquette University Press.

———. 2000. *The Principles of Political and International Law in the Work of Francisco de Vitoria*. Introduction and notes by A. Truyol Serra. Madrid: Cultura Hispánica.

Wells, Donald A. 1967. *The War Myth*. Washington, DC: Pegasus Publishing Company.

White, Kevin, ed. 1997. *Hispanic Philosophy in the Age of Discovery*. Washington, DC: Catholic University of America Press.

Index

About the Author

Dr. Amaya Amell defended her dissertation in May 2012 on "International Law and the Conquest of the Americas: A Critical Reconstruction of the Ideas of Francisco de Vitoria," which reviewed the relationship between colonial expansion and international law. She received her PhD from the Department of Spanish and Portuguese at New York University; her MA from the Department of History at New York University; and her BA from The Ohio State University, where she was a double-major in history and Spanish. Her areas of study, research, and special interests include Spanish language and teaching methodology, Spanish/Latin American literature (especially the Golden Age), early modern European history, colonial history, and the Spanish conquest and post-conquest periods. Dr. Amell has taught at New York University, The Ohio State University, and William Jewell College, where she was an assistant professor of Spanish from 2012 to 2015. Dr. Amell was also an assistant professor of Spanish at the United States Military Academy at West Point from 2015 to 2019 and presently is an assistant professor of Spanish at Millersville University. Her publications include *The Evolution of International Law and Francisco de Vitoria: Justifying Injustice*, published by Lexington Books; "Pedro Páramo y la revolución mejicana" and "Legitimando lo ilegítimo," published by Puente Atlántico; "José María Blanco White. Una figura compleja," published by BookMasters Inc.; and "The Theory of Just War and International Law: From Saint Augustine to Francisco de Vitoria to Modern-Day," published by *Hispanic Journal*.

CPSIA information can be obtained
at www.ICGtesting.com
Printed in the USA
LVHW091611190221
679376LV00006B/85

9 781793 613349